"We miss so many opportunities when public prayers in our churches are ill-prepared, uninformed, scattered, unbiblical, or nonexistent. Pat Quinn has served us immensely by providing a theologically informed, pastoral, Christ-exalting, clear, and insightful book that will serve anyone who has the privilege of leading God's people in prayer. Loaded with examples of actual prayers, *Praying in Public* will make your public prayers more biblical, thoughtful, and God glorifying."

Bob Kauflin, Director, Sovereign Grace Music

"The contemporary church desperately needs to recover a vision for the reformation of the pulpit pastoral prayer. Though well-intentioned, the pastoral prayer too often descends into something that is shallow and ill-conceived and reflects the spiritual poverty of the one praying. Pat Quinn's book is a gold mine of reflection and practical aid to improve the pastoral prayer. I am convinced that if pastors and other leaders follow the instructions given in this marvelous book, congregations are going to be immensely blessed. I believe that many Christians, especially young Christians, learn to pray following the model of the pastoral prayer they hear on Sundays. My prayer is that this book will aid in the reformation of Christ's church."

Derek W. H. Thomas, Senior Minister, First Presbyterian Church; Chancellor's Professor, Reformed Theological Seminary

"*Praying in Public* is a unique book and a very needed book. While we have many books on private prayer, few books walk us through a practical pastoral theology of corporate prayer—praying in public. Pat Quinn not only guides us through seven biblical principles of corporate prayer, he also illustrates these beautifully for us throughout his writing."

Bob Kellemen, Academic Dean, Dean of Students, and Professor of Biblical Counseling, Faith Bible Seminary; author, *Gospel-Centered Counseling*

"As the modern church seeks to reach the present generation, it needs old solutions, not new solutions. Awakening in our day will occur as the church itself is revived. And that reviving will stem from a renewed spirit of prayerfulness. Here is a book to help lead the church down this path upon its knees for its own good and for the good of the world it seeks to reach. Pat Quinn provides practical help and rich examples to ignite prayerfulness in the life of readers and their local church. I have the honor of serving alongside the author at University Reformed Church. I can testify that Pat Quinn can write so adeptly about praying in public because he is a man whose life is suffused with praying in private. He has taught me much over the years and you will find him to be an able guide as well."

Jason Helopoulos, Senior Pastor, University Reformed Church; author, *A Neglected Grace*

"This book delivers on its promise. Any Christian leader with the responsibility of praying in public will discover both guidance and resources in this helpful and instructive book. If you find *The Valley of Vision* useful in preparing for prayer in corporate worship, you'll want this book. I know of no better volume on this important subject."

Donald S. Whitney, Professor of Biblical Spirituality and Associate Dean, The Southern Baptist Theological Seminary; author, *Family Worship*; *Praying the Bible*; and *Spiritual Disciplines for the Christian Life*

"Decades ago, when I was a youth pastor, I had the opportunity to preach at the local Christian high school's chapel services. When the teens had all returned to their classrooms, Pat Quinn sat down with me and gently and pastorally provided me with a much-needed correction to how I approached the passage I had taught. Now I'm a middle-aged pastor, and Pat has done it again, but this time through a book. I encourage you to let this godly pastor sit you down and challenge you to humbly lead your congregation to the throne of grace in prayer."

Noel Jesse Heikkinen, Teaching Pastor, Riverview Church; Regional Executive Director, Acts 29; author, *Unchained and Wretched Saints*

"While Jesus condemned those who parade their private prayer life publicly ('to be seen by men'), he also taught his disciples how to pray rightly in public by both his example and precepts—even as they requested for him to 'teach us to pray.' So with Paul's exhortation—'I desire that in every place the men should pray, lifting holy hands'—I heartily commend this volume as a distillation of biblical insight on how to pray 'everywhere rightly.'"

Harry Reeder, Senior Pastor, Briarwood Presbyterian Church

Praying in Public

Praying in Public

A Guidebook for Prayer in Corporate Worship

Pat Quinn

Foreword by Kevin DeYoung

∷ CROSSWAY®

WHEATON, ILLINOIS

Published in association with the literary agency of Wolgemuth & Associates.

Cover design: Kevin Lipp

First printing 2021

Printed in the United States of America

Scripture quotations are from the ESV® Bible (The Holy Bible, English Standard Version®), copyright © 2001 by Crossway, a publishing ministry of Good News Publishers. Used by permission. All rights reserved.

All emphases in Scripture quotations have been added by the author.

Hymn lyrics are from *Trinity Hymnal* (Suwanee, GA: Great Commission Publications, 1995).

Hardcover ISBN: 978-1-4335-7289-0
ePub ISBN: 978-1-4335-7292-0
PDF ISBN: 978-1-4335-7290-6
Mobipocket ISBN: 978-1-4335-7291-3

Library of Congress Cataloging-in-Publication Data

Names: Quinn, Pat, 1950– author.
Title: Praying in public : a guidebook for prayer in corporate worship / Pat Quinn.
Description: Wheaton, Illinois : Crossway, 2021. | Includes bibliographical references and index.
Identifiers: LCCN 2020049351 (print) | LCCN 2020049352 (ebook) | ISBN 9781433572890 (hardcover) | ISBN 9781433572906 (pdf) | ISBN 9781433572913 (mobi) | ISBN 9781433572920 (epub)
Subjects: LCSH: Prayer—Christianity. | Public worship. | Prayers.
Classification: LCC BV210.3 .Q455 2021 (print) | LCC BV210.3 (ebook) | DDC 264/.1—dc23
LC record available at https://lccn.loc.gov/2020049351
LC ebook record available at https://lccn.loc.gov/2020049352

Crossway is a publishing ministry of Good News Publishers.

VP   30 29 28 27 26 25 24 23 22 21
15 14 13 12 11 10 9 8 7 6 5 4 3 2 1

To Tom Stark, Kevin DeYoung, and Jason Helopoulos—
three beloved pastors who have faithfully
practiced and promoted public prayer

Contents

Foreword

Kevin DeYoung

Acts 6 has long been seen as a great encouragement to preachers. Here you have a pressing need in the church: widows not getting their daily bread and, to make matters worse, the situation looks like ethnic favoritism. And yet, the apostles refuse to be diverted from their calling to preach the gospel. "We will devote ourselves to the ministry of the word!" Teaching the Bible and preaching about Jesus was something that took time—time in front of people and time in preparation. If gospel ministry was meant to happen willy-nilly, the apostles would have waited on tables and squeezed in word work whenever they got the chance. The example of the apostles in Acts 6 reminds us that preaching is a priority in the church, and priorities take time.

But of course, the apostles didn't devote themselves just to the ministry of the word. They also devoted themselves to prayer (6:4). Preaching and praying were the twin turbines providing the church with gospel power. Just like the ministry of the word, the ministry of prayer was something that took time. No doubt, the apostles were thinking mainly about gatherings of corporate prayer like we see in Acts 4. But it's hard to imagine they didn't also have in mind times of private prayer and time spent preparing for prayer. If prayer is to be a vital part of the church, it requires leaders who are not only committed to prayer in their own lives but are also thoughtful and deliberate in how they lead others in prayer. Sustained patterns of rich, biblical corporate prayer don't just happen. They must be planned, and they must be led.

There are lots of good resources available for planning and leading the church in corporate worship. There are books for pastors on how to preach. There are books about leading in song. There are books about how to read Scripture and how to carefully construct a gospel-centered liturgy. Surprisingly, however, there aren't nearly enough books aimed at helping Christians to pray in public. Whether the role is filled by the pastors, or by pastors and elders, or by a worship leader, or by several mature Christians—whatever your context dictates as the right person to pray—surely, that person ought to work hard to think about what and how to pray. We would never dream of getting up to preach unprepared week after week, but in too many churches, that's exactly what we do when it comes to prayer. We have equated a good heart with good prayers and have confused spontaneity with spirituality. There is hardly a church or a Christian out there that couldn't use help in praying more deeply, more biblically, and more thoughtfully in corporate worship.

That's why I am immensely grateful for this new book. I've known Pat Quinn for more than twenty years—as a high school Bible teacher, as an elder, as a biblical counselor, as a worship leader, as a colleague, and as a friend. I had the privilege of serving with Pat at University Reformed Church, and now as the pastor of

Christ Covenant Church I'm honored to commend this excellent volume. Part instruction and part example, this book is a timely resource for pastors, elders, worship leaders, and any Christian who has the privilege of praying in public. Pat gives us seven principles to guide our public prayer, and then gives us dozens of examples from his own public prayer ministry. I heard many of these prayers in person throughout my years in East Lansing, and I can tell you that Pat is as genuine and thoughtful about his public prayers as anyone I know. I'm glad to see the fruit of his labors now in print. Whether you use this book as a pastor in training, as a lay leader in the church, or simply in your own devotional time, I know you will be helped to think more carefully, more biblically, and more doxologically about prayer in the life of the church. May God revive in us once more an apostolic commitment to the word of God and prayer.

Introduction

I will tell of your name to my brothers;
in the midst of the congregation
I will sing your praise.
HEBREWS 2:12

What Would Jesus Do?

For a few years in the 1990s many people found it a helpful physical reminder of their faith to wear a WWJD bracelet. The question "What would Jesus do?" was meant to help us remember Jesus's way of life and then try to do what Jesus would do in our own circumstances. Most of the time that looked like loving our neighbor, forgiving people who hurt us, telling the truth even when it was costly, sharing the gospel, and making courageous moral choices. I wonder, though, how many of us wearing those bracelets thought about doing what Jesus did with regard to prayer?

Prayer was central to Jesus's life and ministry. We get a glimpse into Jesus's personal prayer life in Luke 6:12: "In these days he went out to the mountain to pray, and *all night he continued in prayer to God.*" We see him instructing his disciples about prayer in Matthew 6:9: "Pray then like this. . . ." And in John 6:11 Jesus prayed a familiar mealtime prayer: "*When he had given thanks*, he distributed [the loaves] to those who were seated." We are comfortable with personal prayer, giving thanks for food, and teaching others how to pray, but there is one other kind of prayer Jesus practiced that we may not be as familiar with and which is the subject of this book: congregational or public prayer. Hebrews 2:12 refers to Jesus, saying, "I will tell of your name to my brothers; in the midst of the congregation I will sing your praise." Here is Jesus the worship leader leading the congregation in declaring God's name ("I will tell") and singing his praise ("I will sing").[1]

Jesus fills this worship leader role at the Last Supper as well. As he prays, he:

- *Reveals the Father's name to the disciples to increase their love for him.* "I made known to them your name, and I will continue to make it known, that the love with which you have loved me may be in them, and I in them" (John 17:26).
- *Leads them in a song of praise to the Father.* "And when they had sung a hymn, they went out to the Mount of Olives" (Matt. 26:30).
- *Petitions the Father on their behalf.* "I do not ask that you take them out of the world, but that you keep them from the evil one" (John 17:15); "Sanctify them in the truth; your word is truth" (John 17:17).

---

1   Alistair Begg and Sinclair Ferguson helpfully develop this point in their book *Name above All Names* (Wheaton, IL: Crossway, 2013), 66–67.

If we add to these three elements the petition from the Lord's prayer "and forgive us our debts" (Matt. 6:12), we could define congregational prayer as *public prayer by a Christian leader in which he represents the gathered people of God in adoration, confession, and/or supplication and by which he instructs them in God's ways.* Throughout the Bible we see God working for the good of his people through the representation of duly appointed leaders as they lead, protect, teach, and pray. Besides Jesus, examples of leaders praying for God's people include Moses (Ps. 90: adoration, confession, and supplication), Solomon (1 Kings 8:22–61: adoration, confession, and supplication), Ezra (Ezra 9:6–10:1: confession), Daniel (Dan. 9:1–19: confession, adoration, supplication), and the apostles (Acts 4:23–30: adoration, supplication). All of these prayers both represent and instruct the saints. Representative or congregational or public prayer is thoroughly biblical and, as we will see, has been an important part of Christian worship from the beginning of the church until now. And this has important implications for our worship today.

What Is This Book About?

First of all, this is not primarily a book about prayer in general. There are many wonderful books to help us learn to pray, but the specific topic of this book is congregational prayer.

But this isn't merely a book *about* congregational prayer. Though part 1 looks historically at public prayer and gives guiding principles to follow, this is largely a book *of* prayers. In that sense it's a little like the classic book of Puritan prayers, *The Valley of Vision.*[2] I am not,

---

2 Arthur Bennett, ed., *The Valley of Vision* (Carlisle, PA: Banner of Truth Trust, 2005).

however, a Puritan. I am a twenty-first-century servant of Christ in a PCA church. I am an elder, the Director of Counseling Ministries, and a former worship leader at University Reformed Church in East Lansing, Michigan. Under the leadership of former senior pastors Tom Stark and Kevin DeYoung and present senior pastor Jason Helopoulos, our church has sought to make congregational prayer a regular and robust part of our worship services. I decided to write this book because we believe the Lord has graced us to take this responsibility seriously and to strive to do it as well as we can. My prayer is that this book might stimulate and guide you (and others) to do the same.

We have good reasons to do congregational prayer well. First, it's hard to imagine a worship service without some kind of public prayer. Prayer in the Sunday service is a given, but it is not always done in a clear, concise, and compelling way. The glory of God, the history of the church, and the edification of believers mandate that we take prayer as seriously as other elements of worship, like singing and preaching.

Second, congregational prayer is powerful because God is mighty and has promised to answer our prayers, especially those we ask together (Matt. 7:7–11; 18:19–20). A former pastor once led our congregation in prayer for a little girl facing serious health issues. He prayed clearly, compassionately, boldly, and specifically for her. The congregation was challenged to believe, the parents were encouraged to hope, and, best of all, the prayers were answered!

Finally, good congregational prayer actually models and teaches the congregation how to pray. When the disciples asked Jesus to teach them to pray, he didn't pontificate on prayer—he prayed

(Luke 11:1–4). It's not unusual for people in our church to later ask the one who led in prayer for a copy of the prayer. More than one person has commented that our prayers of confession in particular have helped them confess more intelligently and deeply.

I hope this book will help you and others who might fall into any of these following groups:

- Pastors, elders, worship leaders, and campus and youth workers who desire to lead and pray well over the long haul, but who sometimes feel weary and uninspired and are looking for stimulating, useful, and flexible resources to help.
- Seminarians and interns who are inexperienced in leading worship or public prayer and want a resource to help them plan ahead and grow.
- Seminary professors who want to equip their students for pastoral ministry.
- Growth group or Bible study leaders who desire group prayer to be a regular and vital part of their gatherings.
- Parents who want to revive family worship and lead their families well in prayer.
- Rank-and-file congregants who sometimes find personal prayer tedious, boring, and repetitive, or who might lack confidence and want to be stimulated to fresh prayers of adoration, confession, and supplication.

Let's begin by surveying congregational prayers from church history to see what we can learn about content and practice. I will focus on prayers of adoration, confession, and supplication because, as we will see, these three are the primary types of prayer historically employed in congregational worship.

Liturgies and Prayers of the Church

The Latin Liturgy (Fifth Century)

Adoration: "Glory be to God on high, and on earth peace to men who are God's friends. We praise thee, we bless thee, we adore thee, we glorify thee, we give thee thanks for thy great glory: Lord God, heavenly King, God the almighty Father. Lord Jesus Christ, only-begotten Son; Lord God, Lamb of God, Son of the Father . . . thou alone art the Most High: Jesus Christ, with the Holy Spirit: in the glory of God the Father. Amen."[3]

Confession: "I confess to almighty God . . . that I have sinned exceedingly in thought, word, and deed; through my fault, through my own fault, through my own most grievous fault. . . . Take away from us our iniquities, we entreat thee, Lord, so that, with souls made clean, we may be counted worthy to enter the Holy of holies: through Christ our Lord. Amen."[4]

Supplication: "Deliver us, we pray thee, from every evil, past, present, and to come . . . , be pleased to grant peace in our time, so that with the help of thy compassion we may be ever free from sin and safe from all disquiet."[5]

John Calvin (1545)

Adoration (after the Lord's Supper): "Heavenly Father, we offer thee eternal praise and thanks that thou hast granted so great a benefit

3 Bard Thompson, comp., *Liturgies of the Western Church* (Philadelphia, PA: Fortress Press, 1961), 61.

4 Thompson, *Liturgies*, 57, 59.

5 Thompson, *Liturgies*, 79.

to us poor sinners, having drawn us into the Communion of thy Son Jesus Christ our Lord, whom thou hast delivered to death for us, and whom thou givest us as the meat and drink of life eternal."[6]

Confession: "O Lord God, eternal and almighty Father, we confess and acknowledge unfeignedly before thy majesty that we are poor sinners, conceived and born in iniquity and corruption, prone to do evil, incapable of any good, and that in our depravity we transgress thy holy commandments without end or ceasing. . . . Nevertheless, O Lord, we are grieved that we have offended thee; beseeching thy grace to relieve our distress. O God and Father most gracious and full of compassion, have mercy upon us in the name of thy Son, our Lord Jesus Christ."[7]

Supplication: "Wherefore we pray thee O heavenly Father, for all princes and lords, thy servants, to whom thou hast intrusted the administration of thy justice, and especially for the magistrates of this city . . . for all those whom thou hast ordained pastors of thy faithful people, to whom thou hast intrusted the care of souls and the ministry of thy holy gospel . . . for all men everywhere. As it is thy will to be acknowledged the Savior of the whole world, through the redemption wrought by thy Son Jesus Christ, grant that those who are still estranged from the knowledge of Him . . . may be brought by the illumination of thy Holy Spirit and preaching of thy Gospel to the straight way of salvation."[8]

6 Thompson, *Liturgies*, 208.
7 Thompson, *Liturgies*, 197.
8 Thompson, *Liturgies*, 199–200.

Matthew Henry and the Puritans (1712)

Adoration: "We pay our homage to three that bear record in heaven, the Father, the Word, and the Holy Ghost: for these three are one. We adore thee, O Father, Lord of heaven and earth; and the eternal Word, who was in the beginning with God, and was God, by whom all things were made, and without whom was not anything made that was made. . . . We also worship the Holy Ghost, the Comforter, whom the Son has sent from the Father, even the Spirit of truth, who proceedeth from the Father, and who is sent to teach us all things, and to bring all things to remembrance."[9]

Confession: "Every imagination of the thoughts of our heart is evil, only evil, and that continually, and it has been so from our youth. O how long have those vain thoughts lodged within us! From within, out of the heart proceed evil thoughts; which devise mischief upon the bed, and carry the heart with the fool's eyes into the ends of the earth. But God is not in all our thoughts; it is well if he be in any: Of the Rock that begat us, we have been unmindful, and have forgotten the God that formed us."[10]

Supplication: "We pray, as we are taught, for all men, believing that this is good and acceptable in the sight of God our Savior, who will have all men to be saved, and to come to a knowledge of the truth, and of Jesus Christ, who gave himself a ransom for

9   Matthew Henry, *A Method for Prayer*, ed. J. Ligon Duncan (Fearn, Ross-shire, Scotland: Christian Focus, 1994), 24–25.
10 Henry, *Method*, 36.

all. O look with compassion upon the world that lies in wickedness, and let the prince of this world be cast out, that has blinded their minds. O let thy way be known upon earth, that barbarous nations may be civilized, and that those that live without God in the world may be brought to the service of the living God; and thus let thy saving health be known unto all nations: Let the peoples praise thee, O God, yea, let all the peoples praise thee."[11]

Contemporary Prayers

Adoration: "Indeed, O God, You are love. Your mercies are great. You are compassionate and gracious, slow to anger and abounding in lovingkindness and truth; You keep lovingkindness for thousands, You forgive iniquity, transgression, and sin; and You so loved the world that You gave Your only begotten Son that whoever believes should not perish. . . . We praise Your unfailing love, Father, Son and Holy Spirit."[12]

Confession: "O Lord, God of Abraham, Isaac, and Jacob, be the God of your people today! We confess that we have worshipped all too many other gods. We have devoted ourselves to all too many different values. . . . We confess that we have visited all too many sanctuaries. We have tried to find the sources of life in all too many other places. We thought it was pluralism, but it was the serving of one little Baal after another. . . . We turn to you, and to you alone, to be our God, our only God."[13]

---

11 Henry, *Method*, 103.

12 Terry L. Johnson, ed., *Leading in Worship* (Oak Ridge, TN: The Covenant Foundation, 1996), 27.

13 Hughes Oliphant Old, *Leading in Prayer* (Grand Rapids, MI: Eerdmans, 1995), 108.

Supplication: "O Shepherd of Israel, enthroned on the cherubim, we pray for all peoples. Particularly we pray for street people. . . . We pray for those who are enslaved by drugs, by alcohol, by prostitution and fornication. . . . We pray for the civil authority, for our mayor, . . . for our governor, . . . and for our president. . . . We pray for those in nursing homes. . . . Restore us, O Lord God of hosts!"[14]

Seven Guiding Principles

From this sample of congregational prayers throughout church history we can glean seven principles to guide our own prayers, each of which is explained further in subsequent chapters.

Congregational prayer should aim to accomplish the following:

1. Center on adoration, confession, and supplication
2. Freely use biblical language and allusions
3. Invoke the Father, Son, and Holy Spirit
4. Be thoughtful and reverent
5. Focus on the gospel
6. Have a strong theological foundation
7. Be well-prepared

How to Use This Book

The rest of the book will follow a simple format. Part 1 comprises seven brief chapters that elaborate on and explain each of the seven guiding principles of good public prayer.[15] Part 2 provides

---

14 Old, *Leading in Prayer*, 220–21.

15 The seven principles will often be appropriate for both personal and public prayer, but the emphasis will be on public prayer.

samples of God-honoring prayer to help you pray personally, study, and prepare effective public prayers. The sample prayers are ones I have written and prayed in services at University Reformed Church from 2009 to the present. These prayers can be prayed as is (congregationally or individually), modified to fit specific congregations or needs, or used as models to inspire and guide original prayers.

Again, it is my prayer that this book may contribute to the pursuit of the same excellence in prayer that we instinctively aspire to in other parts of our worship services, such as music and preaching. Paul exhorts us, for the sake of God's glory and the good of the church, to "do your best to present yourself to God as one approved, a worker who has no need to be ashamed, rightly handling the word of truth" (2 Tim. 2:15).

PART 1

SEVEN PRINCIPLES
TO GUIDE PRAYER

1

Adoration, Confession, and Supplication

Stand up and bless the LORD your God from everlasting
to everlasting. Blessed be your glorious name, which is
exalted above all blessing and praise. You are the LORD,
you alone. You have made heaven, the heaven of heavens,
with all their host, the earth and all that is on it, the
seas and all that is in them; and you preserve all of them;
and the host of heaven worships you. . . . But they and
our fathers acted presumptuously and stiffened their neck
and did not obey your commandments. . . . But you
are a God ready to forgive, gracious and merciful, slow
to anger and abounding in steadfast love, and did not
forsake them. . . . Now, therefore, our God, the great, the
mighty, and the awesome God, who keeps covenant and
steadfast love, let not all the hardship seem little to you
that has come upon us, upon our kings, our princes, our
priests, our prophets, our fathers, and all your people,
since the time of the kings of Assyria until this day.

NEHEMIAH 9:5–6, 16–17, 32

Comprehensive Biblical Prayer

This prayer of the Levite leaders of Israel after the wall was rebuilt in Jerusalem is notable in that it contains *adoration* ("Blessed be your glorious name, which is exalted above all blessings and praise"), *confession* ("But they and our fathers acted presumptuously and stiffened their neck and did not obey your commandments"), and *supplication* ("Now, therefore, our God, the great, the mighty, and the awesome God, who keeps covenant and steadfast love, let not all the hardship seem little to you that has come upon us"). As such, it is a good model for those who lead and pray in worship services. The point is not that each prayer needs to include all three but that all three should be the steady diet for worship services. While there are other types of prayers that are appropriate in a service (calls to worship, offering prayers, prayers for illumination, Communion prayers, hymns, benedictions, and specific occasion prayers), they are all variations on these three main types.[1] Let's look briefly at each of these three types of prayer.

---

1 For the purposes of this book I decided to combine praise and thanksgiving into the single concept of adoration instead of following the acronym ACTS—adoration, confession, thanksgiving, supplication—for three reasons. First, the psalms often mix praise and thanksgiving together in the same psalm. An example is Psalm 106:1: "Praise the LORD! / Oh give thanks to the LORD, for he is good, / for his steadfast love endures forever." Second, the historical liturgies quoted in the introduction also frequently mix the categories of praise and thanksgiving in the same prayer. This is true of the Latin rite, John Calvin, Matthew Henry, and contemporary prayers. Third, while the ACTS acronym is very well known and has been helpful to many, my sense is that it is used more often in personal or small group prayer than in corporate worship services. My church, University Reformed Church, has traditionally incorporated prayers of adoration, confession, and supplication into our services.

Adoration

Wholehearted admiration, honor, and love for God are foundational to our relationship with him. They reflect the beauty of his character and the essence of who we were created to be—worshipers. Adoration is the first and most basic kind of prayer. This was especially true before the fall. Imagine the joyful intimacy Adam and Eve experienced with "the LORD God walking in the garden in the cool of the day" (Gen. 3:8) before the awful intrusion of sin. How their hearts would have continually overflowed with glad adoration in the Father's presence and provision.

Even after the disruption of sin, God's grace has motivated countless prayers of adoration throughout history. In fact, we have more reason to thank and praise God as redeemed sinners than if we had never fallen! So it is fitting that the psalms and prayers of the church are full of captivated hearts overflowing with passionate devotion to God. I especially love Psalm 36, where David writes,

> Your steadfast love, O LORD, extends to the heavens,
>> your faithfulness to the clouds.
> Your righteousness is like the mountains of God;
>> your judgments are like the great deep;
>> man and beast you save, O LORD.
> How precious is your steadfast love, O God!
>> The children of mankind take refuge in the shadow of
>>> your wings.
> They feast on the abundance of your house,
>> and you give them drink from the river of your delights.
> For with you is the fountain of life;
>> in your light do we see light. (Ps. 36:5–9)

Two things stir my heart here. One is that David intimately knows and passionately loves a beautiful God. He is intoxicated by the glory of the Lord. Second, David describes this beautiful God with beautiful words. This exquisite imagery not only informs the mind but enflames the heart with adoration. The "sweet psalmist of Israel" (2 Sam. 23:1) is a skillful worshiper and worthy model of adoration.

Confession

If adoration is the most basic and appropriate posture of man before God, confession of sin is the most basic posture for *fallen* man. Since Genesis 3 we cannot rightly think about or approach God except as redeemed sinners.

Several writers have lamented the increasing superficiality of many evangelical worship services. To use an old word, many services lack *gravitas*. Why is this? Of course our entertainment-driven and media-saturated culture bears some of the blame, but I believe there is a deeper reason. Many churches have lost a sense of the holiness of God and the horror of sin. Therefore, corporate confession doesn't seem like an important element of worship. Where is Isaiah's "I saw the Lord sitting upon a throne, high and lifted up" and "Woe is me! For I am lost; for I am a man of unclean lips" (Isa. 6:1, 5)?

We need to be reminded often that sin against a holy God is not merely making mistakes or breaking some rules; it is *blasphemy* (we set ourselves up as rival gods), *treason* (we rebel against the only legitimate authority . . . in wartime!), *adulterous betrayal* (we regularly cheat on our divine bridegroom), *corruption* (our uncleanness stinks to high heaven), and *contempt* (we despise the Lord who created and redeemed us). Sin, both original and actual, is serious and, even though we have been born again and become new creations, we have much to confess every day.

Please understand: this is not to encourage pathological self-hatred or abject despair, but to "come clean" with God (Ps. 51:1–2), to receive afresh his wondrous love and forgiveness (Ps. 130:7–8), and to get on with growing in love for him and our neighbors (Col. 3:12–13). Public confession is an opportunity each week for a congregation of redeemed sinners to get back in touch with reality and revel in the unsearchable riches of Christ. Biblical confession is always done in the context of the gospel and is usually followed by a clear and life-giving assurance of pardon. What a joy to hear "Behold, this has touched your lips; your guilt is taken away, and your sin atoned for" (Isa. 6:7).

So while some would say that including confession in our worship services is negative and damaging to self-esteem, the truth is that without a time of confession, a worship service has no real integrity.

Supplication

This is the relatively easy part, right? Prayers of petition and supplication are the prayers we pray most naturally, both personally and corporately.[2] We know we are needy, and we know God graciously invites us to bring these needs to him (Matt. 7:7–11). Even better, we know he promises to supply all our needs in Christ (Phil. 4:19). So we pray. However, because this kind of prayer comes

---

2   Some think of petition and supplication as different—petition for ourselves, supplication for others. Others see supplication as a more intense form of petition. I treat them as basically synonymous.

so naturally, it is important to make sure our supplications are balanced with adoration and confession. This will keep us from the "grocery list" syndrome of merely praying for our felt needs.

We need to be aware of another prayer imbalance as well. In his book *Speaking Truth in Love*, biblical counselor David Powlison encourages us to pray three types of supplications: prayers to change *circumstances*, prayers to change *us*, and prayers to change *everything*.[3] We could call them circumstantial, transformational, and kingdom prayers. We tend to major in circumstantial prayers (i.e., prayers for healing, travel mercies, marital or work or school issues, etc.), minor in transformational prayers (especially if the circumstantial prayers aren't answered!), and take a pass on kingdom prayers. It's important that public prayer include all three types of supplications for the health of the church and the effectiveness of her mission.

The Lord's prayer in Matthew 6:9–13 is a model of clear, concise, and comprehensive prayer. Notice how Jesus touches on kingdom requests first, circumstantial second, and transformational third.

Pray then like this:

Our Father in heaven,
hallowed be your name.
Your kingdom come,
your will be done,
on earth as it is in heaven.

---

3   David Powlison, *Speaking Truth in Love* (Winston-Salem, NC: Punch Press, 2005), 122–25.

Give us this day our daily bread,
and forgive us our debts,
    as we also have forgiven our debtors.
And lead us not into temptation,
    but deliver us from evil.

Adoration, confession, supplication. Remembering and practicing these three essential types of prayer will protect us from the imbalance that often skews our prayers, promote more mature discipleship, and help leaders "equip the saints for the work of ministry, for building up the body of Christ" (Eph. 4:12).

Reflection

1. Which of the three types of prayer are you most comfortable with? Least comfortable?

2. Read Nehemiah 9, noting all the different topics and themes the Levites developed in this prayer. How could this chapter shape your prayer life this week?

2

Bible-Saturated Prayer

*Prayer, particularly Christian prayer, uses biblical
language. . . . The Bible contains a vast number of
paradigms for prayer and a thesaurus of words to
handle the unique experience of prayer. All this inspires,
encourages, and feeds our experience of prayer.*[1]

*Let the word of Christ dwell in you richly, teaching
and admonishing one another in all wisdom, singing
psalms and hymns and spiritual songs, with thankfulness
in your hearts to God. And whatever you do, in word
or deed, do everything in the name of the Lord Jesus,
giving thanks to God the Father through him.*

COLOSSIANS 3:16–17

1   Hughes Oliphant Old, *Leading in Prayer* (Grand Rapids, MI: Eerdmans, 1995), 7.

Bible Christians

Evangelical Christians are Bible Christians. We want Scripture to inform and shape everything we do. This is how Paul instructs us in Colossians 3:16–17. *Teach* the word, *counsel* the word (admonish), *sing* the word, and *pray* the word (giving thanks). Since the Bible is God-inspired and infallibly guides us into all that is good, true, and beautiful, our public prayers should be saturated with Scripture. We do this by quoting or paraphrasing Scripture in prayer or by alluding to and creatively expressing scriptural themes in prayer. For our purposes we'll call quoting/paraphrasing "scripted" prayer and creative allusion "developed" prayer. Let's look at some examples of and reasons for each.

Scripted Prayer

O Lord, you are the King eternal, immortal, invisible, the only wise God. You are the blessed and only Sovereign, the King of kings and Lord of lords, who alone possesses immortality and dwells in unapproachable light; whom no man has seen or can see. To you be the honor and eternal dominion (1 Tim. 6:15–16).[2]

O let the gospel be preached unto every creature; for how shall men believe in him of whom they have not heard; and how shall they hear without preachers? And how shall they preach except they be sent? And who shall send forth labourers but the Lord of the harvest? (from Mark 16:15; Rom. 10:14–15; Matt. 9:38).[3]

---

2 Terry L. Johnson, ed., *Leading in Worship* (Oak Ridge, TN: The Covenant Foundation, 1996), 22–23.

3 Matthew Henry, *A Method for Prayer*, ed. J. Ligon Duncan (Fearn, Ross-shire, Scotland: Christian Focus, 1994), 104.

There are great benefits to publicly praying "scripted" prayers, whether simply turning Scripture passages into prayer like the above examples, or praying actual biblical prayers such as the psalms or other recorded prayers.[4] The most basic idea is that if we pray God's word, we are praying according to his revealed will and we can be certain he will hear and respond (1 John 5:14–15). This invitation from God to pray the words he has given us is a manifestation of his kindness and a strong foundation for our confidence. Praying God's word also aligns us with his priorities and keeps us from wandering off into inconsistencies or irrelevancies. While we don't want to merely read Scripture in all our prayers, including scriptural quotes or paraphrases will keep us in line and train us to pray weighty and worthy prayers.

Developed Prayer

We have sinned secretly and openly; in thought, word, and deed; ignorantly and presumptuously . . . against thy precepts, promises, and threats; against thy mercies and thy judgments; under thy patience and in thy sight; against our consciences, our purposes, and our covenants; when we were hastening to death and judgment, for which through all our lives we should have prepared.[5]

Lord, Jesus, you have invited us—wretched beggars—to your wedding feast, not only as guests, but as your beloved bride,

---

4 See 1 Kings 8:22–53; Dan. 9:3–19; Eph. 3:14–21; Col. 1:9–14.

5 Richard Baxter, "The Savoy Liturgy," in *Liturgies of the Western Church,* comp. Bard Thompson (Philadelphia, PA: Fortress Press, 1961), 388.

to be united to you in love forever. You are a gracious host and glorious bridegroom and have paid the bride price with your own precious blood. You turn the water of our empty lives into the wine of new life and joy. You refresh and satisfy us with your love. All praise to you Lord Jesus, perfect image of the Father, beautiful Savior, Desire of nations, and coming King.[6]

These prayers capture biblical truths—the inner corruption and outer rebellion of sin, the beauty of Christ's person, and the wonder of his redemptive work—and creatively elaborate on and develop these themes. The goal of developed prayer is to pray biblically and yet relevantly, to express ancient truths in ways that make a fresh impact on the hearers so that they participate in the public prayer with all their heart and soul. A biblically based, creatively developed prayer will have the savor of both timelessness and immediacy. Richard Baxter's prayer above, for instance, is written in seventeenth-century English but could, with minor adjustments, still be prayed today.

A Musical Analogy

Our Director of Music at University Reformed Church, Jon Anderson, gave me an analogy to help me think about these two ways of using Scripture to pray. Jon is an extremely accomplished musician. He is equally adept at playing classical music and jazz, playing the notes as written or taking a theme and developing it through improvisation. Why not learn the classical *and* jazz of leading prayer? While each person who leads in prayer may lean

---

6 See page 92.

more toward scripted or developed prayer, the best way to think about them is to hold them in creative tension: be aware that both are available and that each has its benefits.

Reflection

1. In what ways does the Bible influence the prayers you pray? The prayers you hear in your worship services?

2. What is your favorite prayer in the Bible? Why? When was the last time you actually prayed it to God?

3

Trinitarian Prayer

For this reason I bow my knees before the Father, from
whom every family in heaven and on earth is named,
that according to the riches of his glory he may grant
you to be strengthened with power through his Spirit in
your inner being, so that Christ may dwell in your hearts
through faith—that you, being rooted and grounded in
love, may have strength to comprehend with all the saints
what is the breadth and length and height and depth,
and to know the love of Christ that surpasses knowledge,
that you may be filled with all the fullness of God.

EPHESIANS 3:14–19

In the Name of the Father, Son, and Holy Spirit

Like every other Catholic child growing up in the 1960s, I learned
the sign of the cross as a standard way of beginning prayer. It
involved both action and words. You made a simple motion, first

touching your forehead (saying, "In the name of the Father"), then your chest (". . . and of the Son"), and finally your left and right shoulders (". . . and of the Holy Spirit. Amen."). I confess I hadn't thought about this since I was a boy, but it came back to me as I began this chapter on Trinitarian prayer. If nothing else, I was trained very young to think that prayer involved the Father, Son, and Holy Spirit. This was a gracious gift of God, even though it made little impact at the time.

After decades of reading the Bible, following Jesus Christ, and participating in countless worship services, I am more convinced than ever that prayer is and should be Trinitarian. Of course, this doesn't mean that every single prayer must reference the Father, Son, and Holy Spirit. But for prayer to be truly Christian, it must consistently bear witness to the three-in-one.

The Trinity in Creation and Redemption

The reason prayer is essentially Trinitarian is because, according to Scripture, *everything* is Trinitarian. Genesis 1 and John 1 bear witness to the activity of the Father, Son, and Holy Spirit in creation.

> In the beginning, God created the heavens and the earth. The earth was without form and void, and darkness was over the face of the deep. And the Spirit of God was hovering over the face of the waters. (Gen. 1:1–2)

> In the beginning was the Word, and the Word was with God, and the Word was God. He was in the beginning with God. All things were made through him, and without him was not any thing made that was made. (John 1:1–3)

Second Thessalonians 2:13–14 and other passages similarly show Trinitarian cooperation in the work of salvation.[1]

> But we ought always to give thanks to God for you, brothers beloved by the Lord, because God chose you as the firstfruits to be saved, through sanctification by the Spirit and belief in the truth. To this he called you through our gospel, so that you may obtain the glory of our Lord Jesus Christ. (2 Thess. 2:13–14)

John Frame nicely summarizes the mutual deity and work of the Trinity in creation and salvation: "All three stand together as Creator and Savior. Scripture joins them together in contexts of praise and thanksgiving. They are the ultimate object of the believer's trust and hope. What else can they possibly be, other than one, somehow threefold God?"[2]

The Trinity and Prayer

This Trinitarian mutuality impacts public prayer in two ways. First, each member of the Trinity is intimately involved in the very act of praying. As the old saying goes, we pray to the Father, through the Son, by the power of the Spirit. Paul Miller helpfully elaborates on the mysterious Trinitarian interplay in the act of praying:

> Even now I often don't realize that I am praying. Possibly, it isn't even me praying, but the Spirit. Paul said, "God has sent

---

1   See also Rom. 1:1–6; Gal. 3:10–14; Eph. 1:3–14; Col. 1:3–8; 1 Thess. 1:1–5; Titus 3:4–7.

2   John Frame, *The Doctrine of God* (Phillipsburg, NJ: P&R, 2002), 643.

the Spirit of his Son into our hearts, crying, 'Abba! Father!'"
(Galatians 4:6). The Spirit is not assisting us to pray; he is the
one who is actually praying. He is the pray-er. More specifically, it is the Spirit of *his Son* praying. The Spirit is bringing
the childlike heart of Jesus into my heart and crying *Abba,
Father*. Jesus's longing for his Father becomes my longing. My
spirit meshes with the Spirit, and I, too, begin to cry, *Father*.[3]

While Miller is talking about the Trinity moving us in personal
prayer, the same is true in public prayer. The Holy Spirit moves
leaders to prepare and pray Christlike prayers to the Father on
behalf of his gathered children.

Second, since the Father, Son, and Holy Spirit are equally
divine and essential for our salvation, it makes perfect biblical,
theological, and practical sense that we would refer to each of
them in prayer. Notice how Paul does this in Ephesians 3:14–19.
He prays to the Father that the Ephesians would be strengthened
by the Spirit so that the Son would dwell in their hearts by faith.
This kind of Trinitarian prayer is not simply a formula to follow;
it is the natural movement of a mind instructed in gospel truth
and a heart enflamed by gospel grace.

While the normal practice for Christians is to pray to the Father
through the Son by the power of the Spirit, it is also biblical on
occasion to address Jesus in prayer (John 14:13–14). Praying to
the Holy Spirit (as opposed to "in" the Spirit—see Eph. 6:18;
Jude 20) seems more problematic. There is no biblical precedent
for praying directly to the Holy Spirit, and for good reason. He

3 Paul Miller, *A Praying Life* (Colorado Springs, CO: NavPress, 2009), 64–65.

is the most self-effacing member of the Trinity who loves to point to Jesus and apply his work to our lives. But it is also true that he is equally God and worshiped with the Father and the Son. And as it can be said of the Father and Son, so also of the Spirit: without him we would still be dead in our sins and totally unable to pray at all. Therefore, it is appropriate to praise the Holy Spirit and to occasionally petition him in public prayer. Keith Getty's hymn "Holy Spirit" begins, "Holy Spirit, living Breath of God, breathe new life into my willing soul."[4] Getty's thoughts on the song are relevant to addressing the Holy Spirit in prayer: "'Holy Spirit' is the final hymn I wrote with Stuart Townend as part of the Apostle's Creed album we created in 2005. In this particular song, we desired the hymn to function as a sung prayer about the Holy Spirit's renewing power."[5]

Matthew Henry's prayer of adoration is a good example of Trinitarian prayer:

> We pay our homage to three that bear record in heaven, the Father, the Word, and the Holy Ghost: for these three are one. We adore thee, O Father, Lord of heaven and earth; and the eternal Word, who was in the beginning with God, and was God, by whom all things were made, and without whom was not anything made that was made. . . . We also worship the Holy Ghost, the Comforter, whom the Son has sent from the Father, even the Spirit of truth, who proceedeth from the

---

4 Keith Getty and Stuart Townend, "Holy Spirit" (Getty Music Label, 2019).

5 Keith Getty, quoted in Bob Kauflin, *Worship Matters* (blog), August 10, 2012, worshipmatters.com/2012/08/10/holy-spirit-breath-of-god-gettytownend-hymn/.

Father, and who is sent to teach us all things, and to bring all things to remembrance.[6]

Henry's prayer concisely exalts the Father as the "Lord of heaven and earth," Christ as "the eternal Word . . . by whom all things were made," and the Holy Spirit as "the Comforter . . . sent to teach us all things." The mind is enlightened and the heart enflamed in praise to the glorious three-in-one. This is the goal of good public prayer.

Reflection

1. To whom do you usually address your prayers?

2. What are some modern prayer deficiencies you're aware of that would be cured by more Trinitarian prayer?

---

6 Matthew Henry, *A Method for Prayer*, ed. J. Ligon Duncan (Fearn, Ross-shire, Scotland: Christian Focus, 1994), 24–25.

4

Thoughtful and Reverent Prayer

*Guard your steps when you go to the house of God. To
draw near to listen is better than to offer the sacrifice of
fools, for they do not know that they are doing evil. Be
not rash with your mouth, nor let your heart be hasty
to utter a word before God, for God is in heaven and
you are on earth. Therefore let your words be few.*

ECCLESIASTES 5:1–2

"You Fed Me Breakfast"

Over almost five decades as a Christian I have heard countless
people pray in a variety of settings. While each prayer I heard
was sincere and good, I don't remember many of those prayers.

One particular prayer, however, I remember word for word.
One morning several of us gathered at the church to worship and
intercede for one another and our church. A young man bowed
his head and prayed, "Lord, this morning I woke up with a bad

attitude. And instead of killing me, you fed me breakfast." Why do I still remember this brief prayer, decades later? I believe it is because his attitude was supremely right. He simply acknowledged his sinfulness and expressed his thanks for God's grace. He wasn't sad or depressed; he was amazed. The prayer was humble, reverent, thankful, and brief. Without consciously intending to, he was praying according to Ecclesiastes 5:1–2. His prayer was not the sacrifice of a fool. He wasn't rash. He had a clear sense of who God is and who he was. And his words were few.

A Problem with Our Prayers

I became a Christian in my early twenties out of the 1970s' counterculture with its informal, grassroots, down-to-earth ethos. This ethos permeated everything, from the way we dressed (I was fond of cowboy shirts and patched blue jeans) to the way we worshiped (guitars!) to the way we prayed. I experienced a newfound happy sense of nearness to God that easily expressed itself in colloquial sounding prayer. So far so good. We were created for intimacy with God. However, there was a downside to this informal style of Christianity: the temptation to banality in prayer.

Ironically, the desire to pray fresh, spontaneous, informal prayers can actually backfire. This problem is still with us.

Without a disciplined grounding in Scripture and an intentional effort to think before you pray, it is easy for prayer, especially public prayer, to sound repetitious and even irreverent.

Thoughtful versus Repetitious Prayer

I believe that the more public our prayer is, the more thoughtful it should be. This is especially true when we lead the gathered congregation in prayer. Without some preparation, prayer can easily become repetitious. This can manifest in repeating certain words like *just, um, really, yeah,* the name of God or Jesus, or a pet phrase. Another form of repetition is to repeat themes you've already prayed about in slightly different words, circling and re-circling the runway. Without prior thought we tend to assume, "If I just pray enough words, something is bound to hit," and so we ramble on.

There are two problems with this. First, Jesus warned those who pray against thinking "they will be heard for their many words" (Matt. 6:7). He implies that repetitious prayer may be a prideful attempt to manipulate God. Second, although we don't mean to, we often lose people as we meander in prayer. We don't want congregants to be silently pleading, "Please land the plane!" What might help us be more focused in leading prayer?

God has given us the book of Psalms as our worship prayer book. It is a guide to personal prayer and a model for corporate prayer. We normally think of the psalms as expressing the heights and depths of emotion rather than reasoned discourse, and there is truth to this. However, it's helpful to consider how much thought as well as inspiration went into these prayers. For instance, there are eight acrostic psalms where each verse or stanza begins with a letter from the Hebrew alphabet. One of these, Psalm 111, has ten verses of twenty-two lines, each line beginning with a successive letter of the alphabet. Think about the meticulous planning and skillful crafting this took! The psalmist is able to express reverent praise, helpful instruction, and confident hope all in a brief psalm. These acrostic psalms show that careful thought can express passionate emotion in prayer without repetition or meandering.

Reverent versus Overfamiliar Prayer

Besides the problem of repetitious prayer there also is the problem of irreverent prayer. What causes irreverent prayer? I believe it results from unsuccessfully navigating the various tensions we experience in our relationship with God. These tensions appear in Scripture, exercise our minds, and can affect our prayers.

For instance, Isaiah reminds us that we worship the God of majestic transcendence *and* merciful immanence: "I dwell in the high and holy place, and also with him who is of a contrite and lowly spirit" (Isa. 57:15). That stretches our minds and hearts. It's not easy to hold God's holiness together with his love. So we often try to resolve these tensions by downplaying one side or the other. In my experience, when it comes to the tension between holiness and love, most people would say they prefer God's love. Holiness is hard for us sinful saints. And when we downplay God's holiness in favor of his love, our prayers can reflect that by becoming overfamiliar.

Overfamiliar prayer emphasizes intimacy with God and underemphasizes humble reverence. It forgets the infinite difference between Creator and creature and so addresses the Lord as if "God" were his first name. When this happens, our prayers can sound trite or silly—like saying "Yeah, so God . . ." every third or fourth sentence. But this problem goes deeper than that. It is not honoring to God or spiritually helpful to anyone when the one leading in prayer sounds like God is his homeboy or girlfriend.

No matter the blessings and privileges of gospel sonship—and they are immeasurably great (Eph. 2:7)—congregational prayer should still lead us to trembling joy in the presence of our God of holy love. Our language in prayer should make overfamiliarity and entitlement unthinkable and self-forgetful wonder irresistible.

Martin Luther gives us a brief model of humble, thoughtful, hopeful prayer:

> Teach us, dear Father, not to rely upon or trust in our own good deeds or means, but to venture out upon thine infinite mercy. We commend to thee, heavenly Father, all who strive and work against many grievous anxieties. Strengthen those who still stand. Help raise once again those who have fallen. . . . I doubt not that the things for which I plead will be granted, not because I have requested them, but because thou hast commanded us to pray for them and hast certainly promised them. Amen.[1]

Luther's prayer is tender ("dear Father") and yet reverent ("thine infinite mercy"), humbly dependent and yet boldly confident. Luther's prayer not only models for us how to pray but makes us want to pray. May our public prayers do the same.

Reflection

1. In what situations do you pray in front of others? Where would you place yourself on these two continuums?

Repetitious | | | | | | | | | Thoughtful

Overfamiliar | | | | | | | | | Reverent

2. Who do you know that prays effectively publicly? What makes it effective?

---

1 Martin Luther, *Devotions and Prayers of Martin Luther*, trans. Andrew Kosten (Grand Rapids, MI: Baker, 1965), 45, 65, 67.

5

Gospel-Centered Prayer

And so, from the day we heard, we have not ceased
to pray for you, asking that you may be filled with
the knowledge of his will in all spiritual wisdom and
understanding, so as to walk in a manner worthy of
the Lord, fully pleasing to him: bearing fruit in every
good work and increasing in the knowledge of God;
being strengthened with all power, according to his
glorious might, for all endurance and patience with
joy; giving thanks to the Father, who has qualified
you to share in the inheritance of the saints in light.
He has delivered us from the domain of darkness and
transferred us to the kingdom of his beloved Son, in
whom we have redemption, the forgiveness of sins.

COLOSSIANS 1:9–14

Paul's Obsession

I once heard professor and author D. A. Carson remark that after years of seminary teaching he realized that his students didn't learn all that he taught them, but they did learn what he was excited about. Paul would have agreed with that, and he would have added that he was excited about *everything* he taught. Paul taught by both word and by example. In Colossians 1:9–14 Paul is both praying for the church and teaching us how to pray by his example. Congregational prayer always fulfills both roles. So what can we learn about prayer from Paul in this passage?

The main thing we learn is that the gospel is the "fount of every blessing." Consider the blessings Paul prays for here: knowledge of God's will, being enabled to walk in a way that pleases the Lord and bears fruit, increasing intimacy with the Lord, power to endure hard things with joy, and a final glorious inheritance with the saints in light. What riches! But notice how he ends the prayer with the source and sum of the blessings: "He has delivered us from the domain of darkness and transferred us to the kingdom of his beloved Son, in whom we have redemption, the forgiveness of sins" (Col. 1:13–14). The gospel of deliverance, transfer of kingdoms, redemption, and forgiveness is both the *gateway* and *storehouse* of every good gift (James 1:17). Let's look at some supporting points from Paul's other letters.

The Gospel Is the Gateway

First, without the gospel there is no access to God. Paul says in Romans 5:1–2 that being justified by faith brings peace with God and access into his grace. It's simple: no gospel, no relationship with God and no promise of answered prayer. Praying gospel-centered congregational prayers shows unbelievers that God can't be approached on the basis of their performance, pedigree, or popularity with others. They can approach him only through the blood and righteousness of Jesus Christ. It also reminds believers that their hope of God's favor and mercies is the same blood and righteousness every day. No day are we so good that we don't need gospel grace; no day are we so bad that we should despair of it.

Second, without the gospel, there would be no possibility of blessings, only curses. Deuteronomy 28 recounts the pronouncing of blessings or curses for God's people as they came into the Promised Land. Everything depended on "being careful to do all his commandments" (Deut. 28:1, 15) as they entered the land. In fact, God said curses would fall on them "because you did not serve the LORD your God with joyfulness and gladness of heart" (Deut. 28:47). Not only was obedience required, but joyful and glad obedience! Paul takes up this theme and applies it to us in Galatians 3:10: "For all who rely on works of the law are under a curse; for it is written, 'Cursed be everyone who does not abide by all things written in the Book of the Law, and do them.'" Since none of us comes even close to living up to this standard, we are all under God's eternal curse. No blessings and no hope for any of us. But Paul has been tearing down false hopes only so he can point to the true hope:

> Christ redeemed us from the curse of the law by becoming a curse for us—for it is written, "Cursed is everyone who is hanged on a tree"—so that in Christ Jesus the blessing of Abraham might come to the Gentiles, so that we might receive the promised Spirit through faith. (Gal. 3:13–14)

The gospel brings "the blessing of Abraham" and "the promised Spirit." Or as he says it in Romans 5:18, "justification and life." Ten thousand spiritual and temporal blessings are ours because Jesus became a curse for us. We must continually remind our congregations by the way we pray that the gospel is our only access to God and the only gateway to all his blessings.

But it gets even better.

The Gospel Is the Storehouse

The gospel is not only the "fount of every blessing" in the sense of access or gateway; it is itself the greatest blessing of all. Paul states in 2 Corinthians 4:6 that the gospel is "the light of the knowledge of the glory of God in the face of Christ." If the gospel is the experience of God's glory and if God's glory is the most precious and satisfying thing in the world, then it follows that the gospel gives us what we need and desire the most. There can be no conceivable blessing greater than "the gospel of the glory of Christ" (2 Cor. 4:4). We don't believe the gospel so we can treasure something else more than God. Another way of saying it is that there is no greater delight we can experience than "the love of God in Christ Jesus our Lord" (Rom. 8:39).[1] See how Paul exults in the gospel of the glory of Christ when he says,

> Indeed, I count everything as loss because of the surpassing worth of knowing Christ Jesus my Lord. For his sake I have

---

1   This paragraph is gratefully indebted to the many books, sermons, and articles of John Piper who has helped me and countless others see that God can give us no greater blessing than himself. See especially his books *Desiring God* (Colorado Springs: Multnomah, 2011) and *God Is the Gospel: Meditations on God's Love as the Gift of Himself* (Wheaton, IL: Crossway, 2011).

suffered the loss of all things and count them as rubbish, in order that I may gain Christ and be found in him, not having a righteousness of my own that comes from the law, but that which comes through faith in Christ, the righteousness from God that depends on faith—that I may know him and the power of his resurrection, and may share his sufferings, becoming like him in his death, that by any means possible I may attain the resurrection from the dead. (Phil. 3:8–11)

To use the words of the Westminster Standards, Paul's deepest desire here is to glorify Christ and enjoy him forever: to know him, gain him, be found in him, share his sufferings, and be raised with him.[2]

Leaders must grasp that the gospel is the ultimate prize and that the ultimate prize of the gospel is God himself (John 17:3; 1 Pet. 3:18). If we don't get this, and if our prayers don't help our congregations get this, then we run the risk of inadvertently encouraging a subtle form of idolatry—valuing God's good gifts above the giver (James 4:3–5).

If indeed the gospel is the highest display of the glory of God, the only foundation of the church, and the greatest joy of believers, then our prayers should continually point and lead our congregations to that treasure.

Reflection

1. Read Paul's prayer in Colossians 1:9–14. How are your prayers similar to Paul's? Different?

2. What might help you pray more gospel-centered prayers?

---

2   See the Westminster Shorter Catechism (Q.1) and the Westminster Confession of Faith (26.1).

6

Theological Prayer

He was manifested in the flesh,
vindicated by the Spirit,
seen by angels,
proclaimed among the nations,
believed on in the world,
taken up in glory.
1 TIMOTHY 3:16

Theology: A Dry and Weary Land?

Theology gets a bad rap from some Christians. They believe it is dry, barren, and even divisive. "Doctrine divides!" is the battle cry. This leads to a conscious attempt to keep worship, sermons, and prayer very simple.

While the desire to keep things understandable is good, I see three problems with the antitheology philosophy with regard to public prayer. First, as we discussed in chapter 4, *simple* easily morphs into *simplistic*. Trite and repetitious praises like "Lord, we just want to praise you for your goodness; you are so good all the time, and we don't deserve how good you are to us" say little and promote superficial devotion. Second, without a strong biblical and theological foundation to prayer, you end up praying mostly temporal prayers that don't look much beyond our immediate concerns. Third, nontheological prayers sound narrowly connected to a specific Christian group or subculture and do not build a sense of solidarity with the universal church of Jesus Christ. So how can we move beyond public prayer that sounds trite, temporal, and tribal? One way is to take our cues from Scripture and historic liturgies and creeds to build a solid theological structure for our prayers.

Scripture Soars

The Bible is a precious foundation for prayer. It is unique in being both simple and sublime, rooted in the earth and soaring to the heavens.[1] No promise or prayer is ever trite, either in content or style. As a contrast to the "Lord, you are so good" prayer above, consider Asaph's words with a similar theme in Psalm 73:23–26:

> Nevertheless, I am continually with you;
>   you hold my right hand.
> You guide me with your counsel,
>   and afterward you will receive me to glory.
> Whom have I in heaven but you?

---

[1] This is not to imply that all scriptures are *equally* simple. See 2 Pet. 3:16 for Peter's take on some of Paul's writings.

And there is nothing on earth that I desire besides you.
My flesh and my heart may fail,
> but God is the strength of my heart and my portion
> forever.

Notice the powerful theological truths expressed here: God's sovereignty, omnipresence, guidance, desirability, sustaining grace, and restoration; the believer's faith, hope of heaven, undivided adoration, and humble confidence. All this profound theology and doxology is expressed in a simple, heartfelt, concise, beautiful prayer. This is what the Bible does.

We have so much to learn about prayer from the Bible. Read the psalms often. Study Paul's prayers in Ephesians. Meditate on doctrine in Romans. And daily practice praying Scripture. Since the Bible is God's word, you can take any passage and pray it back to God—even genealogies: "Lord, thank you that you seem to love making lists of your people's names. And thank you that my name is written in the Lamb's book of life!"[2]

Liturgies Last

We looked at several historical liturgies in the introduction to this book. The purpose of this was to remind us that these public prayers of adoration, confession, and supplication have lasted for centuries because they are biblical, weighty, comprehensive, universal, and well-written. I'm not advocating for merely pulling out and using centuries-old liturgies, but

2   I got this idea about praying genealogies from commentator Dale Davis and biblical counselor David Powlison.

I am advocating for studying and learning from them. They have lasted because they express *lasting* perceptions of God's goodness, truth, and beauty as well as *common* human aspirations, hopes, and concerns. Although they were written in a particular time and place, they are still relevant and instructive. They have staying power because they stay rooted and grounded in theological truths. Notice what ministers are instructed to thank God for after the Lord's Supper in the Westminster Directory of Public Worship:

> To give thanks for the great Love of God in sending his Son Jesus Christ unto us; for the communication of his Holy Spirit; for the light and liberty of the glorious gospel, and the rich and heavenly Blessings revealed therein; as namely, Election, Vocation (calling), Adoption, Justification, Sanctification, and hope of Glory.[3]

I suspect that *many* leaders would thank God for his love in sending his Son and *some* might thank him for the gift of the Holy Spirit, but how many would specifically thank God for election, effectual calling, adoption, justification, sanctification, and the hope of glory? Maybe someone who had recently been reading R. C. Sproul or J. I. Packer! But these gospel blessings carry the theological weight of our salvation and hope. They move beyond the temporal to the eternal. Therefore, they should be the foundation of our praises and petitions.

3 Bard Thompson, comp., *Liturgies of the Western Church* (Philadelphia, PA: Fortress Press, 1961), 367.

Creeds Connect

Christian groups tend to develop their own perceptions, concerns, and vocabulary in prayer. How might we move beyond "tribal" prayer—language and content that connects narrowly to our local Christian group? It's not easy to achieve balance between being locally relevant and universally connected.

How do we recognize the universal church as we lead in prayer in a particular time and place? Fortunately, we don't need to reinvent the wheel. Creeds and confessions that have united Christians of almost all persuasions can helpfully inform our prayers. Notice that 1 Timothy 3:16 (quoted at the beginning of this chapter) is an early creed that gave expression to a common faith and unity. Other important creeds followed in the early centuries of the church, the best known being the Apostles' Creed (ca. AD 150). These creeds and confessions are an often untapped treasure.

With countless Protestant denominations in the world, anything we can do in worship to encourage recognition of "one body and one Spirit . . . one Lord, one faith, one baptism, one God and Father of all" (Eph. 4:4–6) is beneficial. Using the ecumenical creeds (Apostles', Nicene, and Athanasian) and Reformed confessions (our denomination, the Presbyterian Church in America, subscribes to the Westminster Confession of Faith) is a powerful way of reminding believers of the essential unity all Christians share.

These creeds can be used in different ways in worship. They can be recited together as part of the service. Although this is not technically prayer, it is a powerful corporate act to confess to God and one another the faith that unites believers through the centuries. Another possibility is that the leader can learn to pray "creedfully." Most simply, this means to pray Trinitarian prayer (see chap. 3) that calls to mind the glory and work of the Father, Son, and Holy Spirit. Since the creeds are Trinitarian in form and accepted by almost all Christians, they remind us that true believers have more that unites them in the gospel than divides them. Praying "creedfully" can be brief yet unifying, as in this section of John Wesley's prayer of adoration and supplication:

> We praise thee, O God: we acknowledge thee to be the Lord. All the earth doth worship thee, the Father everlasting. . . . The Father of an infinite majesty; Thine honorable, true, and only Son; Also the Holy Ghost, the Comforter. . . . O Lord, save thy people, and bless thine heritage. Govern them, and lift them up forever. Day by day we magnify thee; and we worship thy name forever, world without end.[4]

By God's grace we can move beyond trite, temporal, tribal prayer by building a theological foundation for prayer from soaring Scripture, lasting liturgies, and connecting creeds and confessions.

Reflection

1. How would you define theology? What is your honest attitude toward it?

2. This chapter states that "Scripture soars," "liturgies last," and "creeds connect." Which of these do you most want to explore? How could you start?

---

4 Thompson, *Liturgies*, 419–20.

7

Well-Prepared Prayer

Do your best to present yourself to God as one
approved, a worker who has no need to be
ashamed, rightly handling the word of truth.

2 TIMOTHY 2:15

BEFORE WE EXPLORE MORE specific practical instruction in preparing and leading in public prayer, let's quickly review the big themes we've covered so far.

- Adoration, confession, and supplication are the essential components of congregational prayer.
- Biblically scripted and creatively developed prayers are both valid types of prayer.
- Trinitarian prayers honor the person and work of the Father, Son, and Holy Spirit.
- Thoughtful and reverent prayers guard against distracting repetition and dishonoring overfamiliarity.

- The gospel of the glory of Christ should motivate and inform our prayers.
- A solid theological foundation built on love of Scripture, familiarity with historic liturgies, and use of the creeds should undergird our prayers.

An underlying presupposition of these chapters is that effective public prayer must be well-prepared prayer. This is the engine that will move all the other principles. Paul says in 2 Timothy 2:15 that we are to be workmen who have no need to be ashamed in our rightly handling the word of truth. Usually we apply this to preaching and teaching God's word, but it is equally relevant to our praying the word. This chapter briefly explains five general guidelines and then focuses on some specifics of adoration, confession, and supplication.[1]

Five Guidelines for Preparing Congregational Prayer

1. Written and Studied Prayer. Written prayers are exactly that: prayers that are written out ahead of time and read word for word. Studied prayers are prayed from prepared bullet points and so contain more spontaneous prayer. Which is better? My former and present pastors prefer studied prayer. The advantages are that it is organized enough to guard from wandering and repeating and yet free enough to be in the speaker's voice and sound natural. Studied prayer works for those who know the Bible well, are comfortable praying in front of a congregation, and can fluently

---

1   This chapter incorporates several guidelines for public prayer taken from written notes prepared by Kevin DeYoung on leading in prayer, given in a seminar on March 13, 2010, at University Reformed Church. Thanks to Kevin for his kind permission.

"ad lib." Many will prefer this way because it strikes a good balance between form and freedom.

On the other hand, I prefer to write out my prayers ahead of time. The advantage of written prayer is that you have time to carefully craft exactly what you want to say, maximizing the power of striking language and minimizing the possibility of verbally stumbling. However, if you write out your prayer, it's important to remember to write for the ear and not for the eye. You don't want to *sound* like you're reading a prayer, even though you are! It's also important when reading prayers to feel free to add transitional words or phrases and generally embellish so that your reading sounds natural. Whether you pray a written or studied prayer, it is important to practice the prayer ahead of time for maximum familiarity and fluency.

2. Cadence in Prayer. When praying publicly, it's possible to err in praying too fast or too slow. Nervousness often tends toward praying too fast. The words tumble out, sentences run into each other, and the effect is that of a runaway train. People get left behind. However, the opposite problem is also common. Some people tend to slow way down, painfully emphasizing almost every word: "Lord . . . we . . . come . . . before you . . . now . . . in prayer." This kind of prayer plods along unnaturally, and people feel stuck in the mud. We should aim at a normal conversational tone and pace, periodically emphasizing a word or phrase by appropriately varying the volume or speed.

3. Eloquence in Prayer. I realize *eloquence* is a loaded word and that Paul seriously downplayed "lofty speech" in his preaching (1 Cor. 2:1). It would obviously be incompatible with the gospel to try to impress people with our verbal skill or rhetorical power in prayer. Instead, we aim at words that are fluent rather than halting, graceful rather than flowery, clear rather than confusing, and striking rather than trite. Our prayers should flow from and point to God as the source and sum of all that is good, true, and beautiful. This is a high goal but well worth our best efforts. This prayer of John Piper captures the eloquence we aspire to:

> May the power of the Lion and the love of the Lamb make our faith in Christ unshakeable. So deliver us from small dreams and timid ventures and halting plans. Embolden us. Strengthen us. Make us love with fierce and humble love. . . . And in it all, grant that all might see the glory of Christ and that you might be honored through him.[2]

4. Timing of Prayer. The Puritans were known for their long pastoral prayers, sometimes as long as thirty minutes. While we have much to emulate in these prayer warriors of old, we need not aim at half-hour congregational prayers! Our contemporary Christian culture is not ready for that. Start small. Plan to pray three to five minutes. Much can be covered and much good for the soul can be accomplished in a well-prepared prayer of this length.

5. Context of Prayer. Our church uses a worship template created by former pastor Kevin DeYoung. It's helpful to think through the major parts of a worship service and where the different elements fit best. Our service has four main sections that provide a context for the various prayers.

---

2 John Piper, *Seeing and Savoring Jesus Christ* (Wheaton, IL: Crossway Books, 2001), 39.

Praise: includes hymns and songs of praise, responsive reading, creeds, and prayers of adoration.

Renewal: includes prayer of confession, assurance of pardon, songs of response or preparation, offering, baptisms, and a longer congregational prayer of adoration and supplication.

Proclamation: includes prayer of illumination, sermon, and the Lord's Supper.

Response: includes prayer of response, closing song or hymn, and benediction.

Prayers of Adoration

When?

The history of the church shows that prayers of adoration are appropriate at any time during a service but traditionally come during the first part of a service. Many churches have a call to worship at the beginning of a service that contains adoration. An example of a call to worship is Psalm 95:1–4:

> Oh come, let us sing to the LORD;
>> let us make a joyful noise to the rock of our salvation!
> Let us come into his presence with thanksgiving;
>> let us make a joyful noise to him with songs of praise!
> For the LORD is a great God,
>> and a great King above all gods.
> In his hand are the depths of the earth;
>> the heights of the mountains are his also.

These verses can be recited or paraphrased to invite God's gathered people into his presence in worship.

Prayers of adoration can also come during or after a medley of praise songs or hymns. Some worship leaders like to pray transitional prayers of adoration between songs. These can be prepared or spontaneous and sometimes reference the words to the previous or upcoming song or hymn. Our worship leader also usually does a prepared prayer of adoration in the "praise" section of our service.

How?

Mood and Tone: The mood and tone of a prayer should match the subject. Although prayers of adoration, confession, and supplication are addressed to the same Lord, they are not the same subjects. In prayers of adoration aim at "affectionate wonder." We once were spiritually dead, worldly, devil-enslaved children of wrath whom God has eternally loved, made alive, saved by grace, and recreated for good works (Eph. 2:1–10). What undeserved riches!

Scriptural Resources for Prayers of Adoration[3]

Exodus 15:1–18	Psalms 8–9; 18; 21; 23–24;
1 Samuel 2:1–10	27; 29–30; 33–34; 41;
2 Samuel 7:18–24	45–48; 65–66; 68; 75–76;
1 Chronicles 16:8–36	81; 84; 89; 91–93; 95–100;
Nehemiah 9:6–15	103–105; 107–108;

---

3 In this chapter I will suggest various scriptural resources to consult for prayers of adoration, confession, and supplication. However, any passage of Scripture can be turned into any one of these types of prayers by simply using the passage to pray the three R's: Rejoicing (adoration), Repenting (confession), or Requesting (supplication). I learned the three R's years ago in a seminar on prayer by Ben Patterson at University Reformed Church.

111–113; 115–118; 121;
122; 124; 126; 134–136;
138; 145–150

Isaiah 6:1–7; 9:2–7; 25:1–9;
35:1–10; 42:1–4; 53:1–6;
57:14–19; 61:1–11;
65:17–25; 66:10–14

Jeremiah 31:31–34; 32:37–41

Ezekiel 36:25–30

Daniel 6:25–27; 7:9–14

Hosea 14:4–7

Amos 9:13–15

Jonah 2:1–9

Micah 7:18–20

Habakkuk 3:17–19

Zephaniah 3:14–20

Matthew 2:1–12

Luke 1:46–55; 1:67–79

Acts 2:16–41

Romans 8:31–39; 11:33–36

Ephesians 1:1–14

Philippians 2:5–11

Colossians 1:15–20; 2:9–15

1 Timothy 3:16

Titus 2:11–14; 3:4–7

Hebrews 1; 2:10–18;
4:14–16

1 Peter 2:22–25

1 John 3:1–3; 4:9–10

Revelation 4–5; 21:1–22:5

Prayer Writing Exercises[4]

1. Pick one of these three short passages—Psalm 23; Psalm 100; Zephaniah 3:14–17—and do the following:

   - Days 1–3: Read, meditate on, and memorize the passage.
   - Day 4: Write a personal prayer of adoration to the Lord based on the passage. Use "I" in your prayer.
   - Day 5: Write a corporate prayer of adoration based on the same passage. Use "we."

---

4 Numerous sample prayers of adoration, confession, and supplication appear in the second half of this book. It may be helpful to look these over and even pray through some of them as you work on writing your own prayers.

2. Read Psalm 136 and write a corporate prayer recounting the mercies of God in the life of your family or church. Make sure you have a repeating refrain like "his steadfast love endures forever."

3. Read Hebrews 2:10–18 and write out ten bullet points you could use to praise Jesus Christ in a "studied" prayer. Use "you" in the bullet points.

Prayers of Confession

When?

Luke 5:1–11 recounts the story of an encounter between Jesus and Peter that helps us understand the dynamic and timing of conviction and confession. After teaching from Peter's boat, Jesus tells Peter to go out again into the Sea of Galilee and let down his nets for a catch. Peter obeys even though he has been up all night fishing and has not caught a single fish. A fishing miracle occurs, and Peter says to Jesus, "Depart from me, for I am a sinful man, O Lord" (Luke 5:8). The unexpected grace of Christ immediately convicts Peter of his pride and unbelief, and he confesses his sin. The principle here is that encountering the holiness (Isa. 6:1–5) and kindness (Rom. 2:4) of the Lord often leads to confession and repentance. The application here is that a time of confession could very naturally come after a time of hymns or songs of praise. Congregants often experience afresh the goodness of the Lord and a sense of their sinfulness in times of worship, so a worship leader could sensitively lead into a time of corporate confession after encountering the Lord in worship (Ps. 22:3).

Another time for corporate confession is before the Lord's Supper in keeping with Paul's admonition, "Let a person exam-

ine himself, then, and so eat of the bread and drink of the cup"
(1 Cor. 11:28).

How?

Mood and Tone: "Grateful sorrow" captures the appropriate mood
of corporate prayers of confession. How can we not grieve over
our continual foolishness and slowness of heart to believe (Luke
24:25)? How can we not rejoice in the Father's continual forgiveness, love, and redemption freely given us in Christ (Ps. 130:4,
7–8; Rom. 8:31–39)?

Confession of what? For confession to be thoroughly biblical, it
must address both *original* sin (Gen. 6:5; Ps. 51:5; Jer. 17:9; Rom.
1:18; 5:12; Eph. 2:1; 4:17–18) and *actual* sin (Rom. 1:21–32;
3:10–18; 1 Cor. 6:9–10; Gal. 5:19–21; 2 Tim. 3:1–7; James
4:1–12; 2 Pet. 2:1–22); sins of the *heart* (Ezek. 14:1–6) and sins
of *behavior* (Eph. 4:25–5:12; Col. 3:5–8).

Assurance of forgiveness: It is important that in most cases, confession of sin is followed by an assurance of God's pardon flowing
from Christ's redemptive work. This leads back to the glory of
God's grace in the gospel and turns the sorrow of confession into
the joy of forgiveness. One commonly used assurance is 1 John
1:8–9: "If we say we have no sin, we deceive ourselves, and the
truth is not in us. If we confess our sins, he is faithful and just
to forgive our sins and to cleanse us from all unrighteousness."

Scriptural Resources for Prayers of Confession

Exodus 20:1–17	Psalms 6; 32; 38; 51; 130; 143
Nehemiah 9:16–38	Proverbs 6:16–19; 29:20–25
Job 42:1–6	Isaiah 6:1–7

Ezekiel 14:1–6; 34:1–6

Daniel 9:3–19

Amos 6:8

Malachi 1–3

Matthew 5–7

John 6:25–41

Romans 1:18–32

1 Corinthians 6:9–11, 13:1–7

Galatians 5:16–21

Ephesians 4:25–5:21

Colossians 3:5–11

1 Timothy 6:3–10

2 Timothy 3:1–5

Hebrews 3:7–19

James 1:19–27; 2:1–26; 3:13–15; 4:1–12; 5:1–6

1 John 2:15–17

Revelation 2–3

Scriptural Resources for Assurance of Forgiveness: Psalms 32:1–5; 51:17; 130:3–8; Jeremiah 31:33–34; Ezekiel 36:25–29; Micah 7:18–20; Zechariah 3:1–7. Any gospel passage can be turned into an assurance of forgiveness, such as Romans 3:23–25; 5:1–11; 8:31–39; Galatians 3:13–14; Ephesians 2:4–10; Philippians 3:8–9; Colossians 2:13–15.

Prayer Writing Exercises

1. Using Exodus 20:1–17, write a corporate prayer of confession based on the Ten Commandments. Include an assurance of pardon.

2. Look over the Beatitudes (Matt. 5:2–11) and write out a responsive reading for corporate confession. After each specific point of confession, have a repeated refrain such as "Lord, forgive our sins and cleanse our hearts."

3. Read Jesus's letters to the churches in Revelation 2–3 and write out ten bullet points for a corporate prayer of confession. Practice praying it until it feels natural and fluent.

Prayers of Supplication

When?

Prayers of supplication, often part of what the Protestant tradition calls the *pastoral* or *long prayer,* have historically come sometime before the sermon. Our church calls this the *congregational prayer,* and it often comes right after the offering. Since there is a prayer of confession previous to this in our services, it usually includes both adoration and supplication and is often followed by a song or hymn before the sermon. Prayers of supplication could come after the sermon and tie in to sermon points, but in that case the prayer should be kept shorter as people have already been listening for a long time.

How?

Mood and Tone: Prayers of supplication should have a tone of "urgent confidence." We pray urgently (Luke 18:1–8) because as dependent creatures we cannot ultimately protect, sustain, or provide for ourselves. We desperately need the mercies of God for body and soul every moment of every day.[5] We pray confidently because, in Christ, God is our loving heavenly Father who promises to meet our needs and more.[6]

What to Pray For: Here are some possible models for prayers of supplication.

1. The early church and the Reformers prayed for four areas.

- Civil authorities (1 Tim. 2:2)
- Christian ministry (Matt. 9:36–38; 1 Tim. 2:1–2)

---

5   See Num. 6:22–27; Deut. 6:10–12, 8:1–10; Pss. 81; 136; John 15:4–5; Phil. 4:19.
6   See Ps. 37:4; Matt 6:25–34; 7:7–11; John 15:7; 2 Cor. 9:8.

- The salvation of all people (1 Tim. 2:1–4)
- The afflicted (2 Cor. 1:3–4)

2. Pray "inside out."

   - Your own congregation: pastors and staff, ministries, missionaries, congregational needs
   - Other gospel-centered churches in your area
   - Your city: businesses, schools, city government, police, safety
   - Your state: leaders, state needs
   - Your country: leaders, domestic and foreign concerns, justice issues, and so on
   - The world: trouble spots, the persecuted church, natural disasters, and so on

3. Pray David Powlison's three types of prayers.

   - Circumstantial (illnesses, jobs, family relationships)
   - Transformational (holiness, perseverance in trials)
   - Kingdom (gospel ministry, the world)

4. In praying for your own congregation, you can pray for things like the sick, new marriages, births, and deaths by name (unless you know that someone doesn't want to be mentioned publicly). But other needs should be prayed for more generally (e.g., struggling marriages or families). You want to create a climate where people know leaders are concerned about individuals without creating the expecta-

tion that every congregational need will be prayed for by name every week.

Scriptural Resources for Prayers of Supplication:

1 Kings 8:27–53	Daniel 9:16–19
Nehemiah 9:32–38	Jonah 2:1–9
Psalms 7; 10; 13; 17; 20; 22;	Matthew 6:7–15; 7:7–11
25; 28; 31; 35; 39; 42–44,	John 15:1–11; 17:1–26
55–57; 59; 61; 69–71; 74;	Acts 4:23–31
77; 79–80; 83; 85–86; 88;	Ephesians 1:15–23; 3:14–21
90; 109; 119; 121; 132;	Philippians 4:4–7
140–142	Colossians 1:9–14
Lamentations 3:1–21	Hebrews 13:1–21

Prayer Writing Exercises

1. Use Colossians 1:9–14 to write a corporate prayer of adoration and supplication for your group or congregation. It can be a written or studied prayer. Fit it to your specific group and pray it for them in your personal prayer time.
2. Pick a favorite passage of Scripture and pray through the three R's (rejoicing, repenting, and requesting) with your spouse, family, Bible study, or ministry team (see footnote 3).
3. Read and pray through several of the sample prayers in part 2 of this book. Now try your hand at writing a congregational prayer for your congregation that includes adoration, confession, and supplication.

SAMPLE PRAYERS

8

Prayers of Adoration

"BLESSED BE THE GOD and Father of our Lord Jesus Christ! According to his great mercy, he has caused us to be born again to a living hope through the resurrection of Jesus Christ from the dead, to an inheritance that is imperishable, undefiled, and unfading, kept in heaven for you, who by God's power are being guarded through faith for a salvation ready to be revealed in the last time" (1 Pet. 1:3–5).

We delight in you, heavenly Father. We know that your greatest joy is to be the God and Father of our Lord Jesus Christ. How happy you are in your beloved Son: the radiance of your glory, the perfect expression of your holy love, the true prophet, the great high priest, the good shepherd who lays down his life for the sheep.

We praise you that you don't merely tell us we must be born again; you *cause* us to be born again through the resurrection of Jesus from the dead. We could never raise our hearts from the deadness of our rebellion unless you enabled us and drew us to Jesus. Thank you for the *living hope* we have of a glorious inheritance: a new heaven and earth where righteousness dwells;

imperishable and immortal bodies; perfected spirits free from the corruption of sin; and an eternity of happiness with you and all your children. This living hope sustains us each day as we navigate through the pleasures and pains of life.

We praise you that you not only keep this inheritance safe for us in heaven but you guard us as well on earth by your mighty power. You are a strong refuge of security in this broken and hostile world where people seek security in their fragile relationships, temporary vocations, fleeting possessions, and overrated accomplishments. Thank you that our future is rock solid and eternally glorious and all-satisfying in Christ. In Jesus's name. Amen.

———

Lord, we praise you for your excellent greatness and abundant goodness! It is our delight to drink from the living waters of your grace. We praise you that your grace is undeserved and powerful, forgiving and transforming, majestic and merciful. We praise you that your grace has appeared in the coming of your Son and has brought salvation for all men and women, for all boys and girls, for all who look to Jesus in faith. We are here this morning because of your saving grace. Some may be encountering it for the first time; others can't even count the times. But we praise you that your grace is sweet and strong, your steadfast love better than life.

We praise you for the powerful effects of your grace: it saves us from the wilderness of sin and death and leads us to the Promised Land of righteousness and life. It teaches us to say no to deceitful pleasures, degrading habits, and dishonorable attitudes. It empowers us to live lives of joyful freedom, winsome integrity, and Christ-honoring love.

Thank you, Father, for the power of Jesus's death and resurrection, which frees us from all attempts to do life on our own and sets us apart to follow him in doing good works that glorify your great name.

Thank you that, by your grace, you lift our eyes up beyond this world of seductive distractions and deadly counterfeits to the only one who is worthy of our worship and able to satisfy our deepest longings.

And so we look up right now and say, "Come, Lord Jesus, come!" You are our blessed hope. You are our coming King. You are our returning bridegroom. We long for you to come in glory, abolish all evil, and take us home to glorify and enjoy you forever. We pray in your matchless name. Amen.

———

"O LORD, my heart is not lifted up; / my eyes are not raised too high; / I do not occupy myself with things / too great and too marvelous for me" (Ps. 131:1).

Yahweh, you are the great unchangeable "I AM," the one who created all things for your glory and who delights in your own perfections in your beloved Son. You need nothing from us but, rather, you give life and meaning to each one of us. Everything we are and have is your gift to us, and we love to praise you for your sovereign grace.

We humble ourselves before you. We must not and will not exalt our own thoughts, opinions, desires, or ambitions above you.

We must not and will not set our affections on anything besides you. In your presence is fullness of joy and at your right hand are pleasures forevermore. We must not and will not exalt ourselves above you lest we be consumed in our pride. Your thoughts are higher than our thoughts and your ways higher than our ways. Instead, we will trust in and submit to your word and worship you as our almighty, sovereign, glorious, and gracious Father.

"But I have calmed and quieted my soul, / like a weaned child with its mother; / like a weaned child is my soul within me" (Ps. 131:2).

Lord, as we draw near in humble adoration, we love the calm and quiet joy you give us. Like a weaned child we seek the intimacy of worship and let go of our fretful demands for worldly comfort, success, control, and vindication. We surrender our anxious fears about our marriages, children, finances, health, careers, and ministries. We will follow you as you lead us beside the quiet waters of restful trust.

"O Israel, hope in the LORD / from this time forth and forevermore" (Ps. 131:3).

O church, beloved children of God, cast your cares upon him who cares for you. He who did not spare his own Son, but gave him up for us all, how will he not also with him graciously give us all things? Put your hope in him today, tomorrow, and forevermore. Through Christ our Lord. Amen.

———

O great God of highest heaven, we enter into your gates with thanksgiving and into your courts with praise! Our hearts are full of the sights and sounds and songs of this Christmas season.

Father, we praise you for the holy hush of winter, when the whole creation waits silently for the birth of new life. We praise you for this celebration of the incarnation, when our earthly darkness was pierced by your heavenly light, when the Creator of worlds became a nursing babe, when our Sovereign Lord became our suffering servant, and when the heart of all love became a man. Most of all we praise you for the glory of your grace in Christ. All is grace from first to last.

In grace, through Christ, you have visited and rescued us from this present evil age, raised up a banner of salvation for us, saved us from our enemies so that we might serve you without fear, forgiven us our countless and grievous sins in your tender mercy, sent the sun of righteousness to end the night of sin, given light to those who stumble in the dark, and led us into the path of peace

Thanks be to you, heavenly Father, for your indescribable gift! We pray in Christ's name. Amen.

———

Heavenly Father, on this Sunday morning, we praise you for creating the abundant greenery, longer days, and warmth and beauty of summer. These are all testimonies of your goodness and generosity and a foretaste of heaven.

Thank you for all that our five senses experience of your glory: the taste of grilled meat, the orange and blue and red of sunsets, the singing of birds and chirping of insects, the tenderness of children's hugs, the smell of flower gardens, and a thousand other innocent sensual pleasures.

We marvel at the glory of your creation and the greater glory of your character. The Rocky Mountains are weightless compared to your majesty; the Pacific Ocean is miniscule compared to your immensity; meadows of wildflowers are pale compared to your beauty; exploding stars are feeble compared to your power; roaring lions are tame compared to your wildness; marital passion is a kindergarten crush compared to your love for us. In a word, you are holy: the source and sum of all that is good, true, and beautiful. You are high and lifted up, unsearchably great, transcendently majestic, infinitely perfect, a consuming fire of righteousness.

As we consider your holiness, Lord, we tremble before you and close our mouths in holy fear. You are not like us; you are the Lord. You owe us nothing; you are the Lord. We deserve your righteous displeasure, rebuke, and curse. You are the Lord.

And yet, you are gracious and merciful, slow to anger, and abounding in steadfast love. You are unfailingly good to each one of us, and your mercy never ends.

We know that this amazing grace is not self-evident; it is not deserved; and it is found only in your Son Jesus. He was punished so we could be forgiven; treated as a blasphemer and traitor so we could be blessed as worshipers; executed as a criminal so we could receive a son's inheritance; and crushed with pain so we could taste joy and pleasure forever. This is grace. This is the gospel. This is our hope and joy and very life. In Jesus's name. Amen.

"For God, who said, 'Let light shine out of darkness,' has shone in our hearts to give the light of the knowledge of the glory of God in the face of Jesus Christ" (2 Cor. 4:6).

Lord, this is what it means to be converted, to be born again, to be saved, to be a Christian—to see your eternal glory in Christ with eyes of faith. Even a glimpse radically changes us from idolaters to worshipers, from slaves of sin to sons of God. How we thank you for the beauty of your Son. He is the fairest of ten thousand, the bright morning star, the desire of nations. And now, with one heart and mind we worship him who is altogether:

Lovely in his birth and incarnation. Though he was rich, for our sakes he became poor, shared the vulnerability of our flesh and blood, was born of woman, and was made under the law for our sakes.

Lovely in the whole course of his life. He was perfect in his holiness and obedience, and the depth of his poverty and persecution was unmatched. He willingly was cursed so we could be blessed.

Lovely in his death. He was bruised and broken on the cross, hated by man, and forsaken by God. He destroyed the power of Satan and sin by his sacrificial death and turned away God's just wrath.

Lovely in his glorious resurrection. He conquered death by his indestructible life, assured us of our forgiveness and acceptance, vindicated his work, glorified the Father, and brought life and immortality to light through the gospel.

Father, we know that we please you the most when we are most pleased with your Son, our mediator, King, and brother. We adore him as the radiance of your glory and the exact imprint of your nature. We pray with gratitude in his name. Amen.

———

Father, we exalt you that you are the:

Creator of all things visible and invisible: of planets and stars and galaxies and wonders that stagger our imaginations; of the power of a tropical storm and the peace of a summer evening; of blazing autumn colors and cold winter nights; of babies and birthdays, friends and family, and all things that reveal your glory.

King of kings who rules over every molecule of space in the universe and every second of time in history to bring about your good purposes. You care for and command everything in your creation. You reign over all things in absolute wisdom, power, majesty, and love. You have compassion on all you have made and satisfy the desire of every living thing.

Judge of the living and the dead. You are the Holy One to whom every person will give an account for his life. You judge not only our actions but the intentions of our hearts by your holy word. You will give to people according to their works: you will give eternal life to those who, by patience in well-doing, seek for glory and honor and immortality; you will give wrath and tribulation and distress to those who are self-seeking and do not obey the truth.

God and Father of our Lord Jesus Christ, the Father of mercies and the God of all comfort. You show compassion to your own children. You know our frame and remember that we are but dust; you forgive all our sins because of Jesus's death and resurrection; you give us each day our daily bread and provide for all our needs; and you give good gifts to your children, especially the Holy Spirit to those who ask. For all these blessings and countless more we give you praise. In Jesus's name. Amen.

"It is good to give thanks to the LORD, / to sing praises to your name, O Most High; / to declare your steadfast love in the morning, / and your faithfulness by night, / to the music of the lute and the harp, / to the melody of the lyre. / For you, O LORD, have made me glad by your work; / at the works of your hands I sing for joy" (Ps. 92:1–4).

It is good to give thanks to your name, O Lord our righteousness, our wisdom, our glory, our hope, our exceeding joy! We delight in your steadfast love and faithfulness to us. You have truly made us glad by your works of glorious creation, sustaining providence, and gracious redemption. We worship you, Father, for being the author of all things in heaven and earth. All things are yours, and you rule over all things by your sovereign grace.

We praise you, Jesus, for being the perfect image and radiance of the Father, the firstborn of all creation, the head of the church, the fairest of ten thousand, and the Savior of the world.

We adore you, Holy Spirit, the giver of life, the Comforter and Helper, the Spirit of wisdom and understanding, counsel and might, knowledge and the fear of the Lord.

It is good to give thanks and praise to you, Lord, because you are supremely worthy and because it is our highest joy to praise you. Thank you for blessing each of us far more than we deserve and for blessing our church community in countless way. You truly make us glad by your works. We give you thanks in Jesus's name. Amen.

———

God of glory, Abba, Father, we join angels, apostles, prophets, martyrs, and all the saints in heaven and earth in offering you endless praise. You alone have life in yourself. You are infinite in majesty, powerful in sovereignty, awesome in holiness, incomprehensible in wisdom, terrible in judgment, tender in compassion, and wondrous in salvation. We praise you for the glory of your grace in Christ—you have chosen us, drawn us to Christ, forgiven our sins for his sake, made us alive in him, and promised us eternal life. You are truly good, your steadfast love endures forever, and we love you with all our hearts.

Lord Jesus, you have invited us—wretched beggars—to your wedding feast, not only as guests, but as your beloved bride to be united to you in love forever. You are the gracious host and glorious bridegroom and have paid the bride-price with your own precious blood. You turn the water of our empty lives into the wine of new life and joy. You refresh and satisfy us with your love. You open our blind eyes to the greatness and beauty of your majesty. You died for our sins and crucified our old selves. You conquered our dark desires and destroyed death itself. All praise to you, Lord Jesus, perfect image of the Father, beautiful Savior, desire of nations, and coming King.

Holy Spirit, together with the Father and the Son you are truly God—Lord and giver of life, bestower of gifts, Comforter, counselor, advocate, and Helper. How grateful we are for you. We could not live one moment without your tender mercies. You are life to our souls and healing to our flesh through the word. You inspire, illuminate, and apply the Scriptures to our lives. You reveal Jesus and bring us to the Father through him. May we never grieve you, always honor you, respond quickly to your influence, and bring glory to the Father and the Son. We pray all this in the name of the triune God. Amen.

———

Father, long ago you said to Abraham, "Fear not, . . . I am your shield; your reward shall be very great." We thank you this morning that through the gospel of your Son we too are participants in this blessing of Abraham. We praise you for your very great reward of your daily protection and the security it gives us; the pleasure of fellowship and worship with brothers and sisters; the overflowing generosity and kindness you show us in countless ways; opportunities to serve you creatively and joyfully; and the glorious inheritance of immortal bodies, a new heaven and earth, and ever-increasing joy in your presence.

Father, all this grace is staggering and leaves us breathless with wonder! We worship and adore you, triune God. All that we are and have are your gifts. You alone are worthy of all praise, honor, and glory. Father, yours is the kingdom, the power, and the glory. Jesus, you are the desire of the ages and the King of kings. Holy Spirit, you are the Lord and giver of life, our Helper and counselor and Comforter. It is good to give thanks to the Lord, to sing praise to your name O Most High, for you are good and your steadfast love endures forever. Amen and Amen!

———

"Praise the Lord! / I will give thanks to the Lord with my whole heart, / in the company of the upright, in the congregation. / Great are the works of the LORD, / studied by all who delight in them. / Full of splendor and majesty is his work, / and his righteousness endures forever" (Ps. 111:1–3).

Our heavenly Father, we give you praise for the greatness and splendor and majesty of your works.

We praise you for your works of creation, for the changing of the seasons, for wind and rain, for fields and forests and the wildlife that live there, for ten thousand physical beauties and our five senses to enjoy them. Truly Lord, your glory fills the earth, and we give you praise.

We praise you for your works of providence. You rule with sovereign authority over planets and atoms, nations and neighborhoods, families and each person here today. Without your will not a bird can fall from a branch or a hair can fall from our heads. We praise you that you work all things—no exceptions—for our good: marriage and singleness, neighbors and coworkers, best friends and worst enemies, wealth and poverty, strengths and weaknesses, health and sickness, spouses and children, sins we've committed and abuse we've suffered, blessings we've enjoyed and tragedies we've endured, all our wise and foolish choices. All these things must serve your purpose of conforming us to the image of Christ for his everlasting glory and our everlasting joy.

We praise you for your greatest work—the gospel of the glory of Jesus. He is the Word of God, the one through whom and for whom all things were created, the first and last and living one, the fairest of ten thousand, the Holy One, the King of kings, the good shepherd, the bridegroom, the great high priest, and the final sacrifice for our sins. In the fullness of his grace we praise you in his name. Amen.

—

Joy to the world! The Lord is come:
let earth receive her King;
let every heart prepare him room,
and heaven and nature sing.[1]

Lord, how this world is starved for joy and seeks it in tinsel treasures and poisonous pleasures! Thank you that when you sent Jesus, you sent the only real and lasting joy.

With great anticipation and hope we joyfully receive Christ now. We have prepared our hearts and once again receive him as our Savior from sin, Lord of life, lover of our souls, closest friend, brother in the fellowship of suffering, and as the very meaning and purpose of our lives. We have sung your praises and we sing in our hearts now—"Joy to the world! The Lord is come!"

Joy to the earth! The Savior reigns:
let men their songs employ;
while fields and floods, rocks, hills, and plains
repeat the sounding joy.

We praise you Lord, that the Savior reigns—the stone that the builders rejected has become the chief cornerstone. The suffering

---

1   "Joy to the Word," Isaac Watts, 1719.

servant has borne our sorrows and griefs and sicknesses and pains. The curse bearer has become the blessing giver. The sun of righteousness has risen. Thank you that the joy of our salvation is not only for us but for extended family, neighbors, coworkers—for the whole world. You call us to go across the street, across the aisle, across racial divides, and across the world to bring the joy of our salvation.

We praise you that the salvation Jesus brings impacts the entire creation—fields and floods, rocks, hills, and plains repeat the sounding joy. The oceans will roar, the trees of the field will clap their hands, the mountains will bow down when the King of glory comes. One day every knee will bow before Jesus and every blade of grass will be renewed to bring praise to him. In this glorious hope we pray. Amen.

———

"First of all, then, I urge that supplications, prayers, intercessions, and thanksgivings be made for all people, for kings and all who are in high positions, that we may lead a peaceful and quiet life, godly and dignified in every way. This is good, and it is pleasing in the sight of God our Savior, who desires all people to be saved and to come to the knowledge of the truth. For there is one God, and there is one mediator between God and men, the man Christ Jesus, who gave himself as a ransom for all, which is the testimony given at the proper time" (1 Tim. 2:1–6).

Heavenly Father, we praise you that you are:

The one true God. All the false gods of our culture and all the trivial idols of our hearts are imposters and less than nothing.

Immortal, invisible, God only wise, you alone are holy, high and lifted up, exalted above the heavens, awesome in majesty, terrible in judgments, tender in mercy, compassionate to all you have made. We worship you as the Creator and ruler over all things in heaven and earth.

God our Savior. The world looks to many things to bring the "good life"— presidential candidates and party platforms, media polls and political pundits, better education and affordable housing, personal freedoms and civil rights, investment strategies and retirement accounts, psychological therapies and self-help books. While we thank you for many of these common grace gifts, not one of them can save! Only you can see clearly what ails us and cure deeply what destroys us.

Lord Jesus, we praise you that you are:

The one mediator between God and men. You alone are the way, truth, and life and no one comes to the Father but through you. There is no one else who is truly God and truly man. No one else has lived our life and died our death. No one else fully understands our humanity and has power to transform it. How amazing, how wonderful that you gave yourself up for us to be a ransom for all. Hallelujah, what a Savior! Amen!

———

Our Father and our God, all honor and glory belong to you. In the beginning you created the heavens and the earth; you sustain them now by your providence, and you direct them to your glorious purpose. We know you did not act alone. Before you created the world, your Son was with you and was like you—God of God;

light of light; very God of very God. You created all things through him and for him. He was at your side as your daily delight. We marvel at his deity and creative power. Every blade of grass bears his imprint; every work of human genius testifies to his glorious greatness. We have come to understand, Lord, that we can actually see your glory in his face. So, in his name we come, and in his Spirit we lift up our praises to you.

We confess our faith in your Son, Father. We believe that Jesus is the true light that enlightens every person, the one and only sacrifice for our sins, the resurrection and the life, the ruler over all things, the sanctifier and sustainer of the church, the warrior King, and the coming bridegroom. We sadly acknowledge, Lord, that many people ignore and resist the knowledge of your saving grace in Christ and refuse to come to him that they might find forgiveness and eternal life. It was that way when he walked the earth, and it is still the same today. It will always be so unless you intervene. Thank you for your promise that to each person who receives Jesus Christ and believes in his name, you give the right to become your child. What a marvelous thing! People today hope against hope that their sins and failures will be forgiven. They ache to belong and to be loved. They long for deep and lasting change. And they fear what the future will bring. O how precious is your promise to freely forgive, to change them into holy people, and to bring them to the happiest of all happy endings. We thank you for this blessed hope in Jesus's name. Amen.

"Blessed be the Lord God of Israel, / for he has visited and redeemed his people . . . that we, being delivered from the hand of our enemies, / might serve him without fear, / in holiness and righteousness before him all our days" (Luke 1:68, 74–75).

Lord, when you look down upon this earth, you see a world that has turned away from you, rebelled against your rule, spurned your love, and been indifferent to your glory. Truly we are fallen and deserving of your fierce anger and judgment. Yet you have not stood far off in disgust or come to destroy us. You have graciously visited us in person and redeemed us through your Son, Jesus Christ. He took on our very humanity, shared in all our joys and sorrows, suffered unspeakably, and died horrifically for us on the cross—all so that we might serve you without fear, in holiness and righteousness all our days.

Thank you for saving us from our enemies: a fallen world that continually entices us to sin, our corrupt flesh that weighs us down like a millstone, and a cruel adversary who wants only to steal our faith, kill our joy, and destroy our lives.

Thank you that you have pardoned us freely, counted us righteous, adopted us as your beloved children, crucified our old nature, and raised us to new life—all in Christ. It is our greatest joy to serve you gladly and wholeheartedly as you call us and equip us for good works. In Jesus's name. Amen.

"Blessed be the God and Father of our Lord Jesus Christ, the Father of mercies and God of all comfort, who comforts us in all our affliction, so that we may be able to comfort those who are in any affliction, with the comfort with which we ourselves are comforted by God" (2 Cor. 1:3–4).

We praise you that you are God. You are totally self-sufficient, not needing anything from us. You give us life and breath and everything else out of the infinite abundance of your grace. You are majestic and mighty and merciful and mindful of each one of us. You are the Creator and sustainer and Redeemer of all things.

We exult you that you are Father. You know that we are dust, yet you show us compassion. You know each one of your children by name. You know when we rise up in the morning and lay our heads down at night. You know what we will think, say, and do—not only today but tomorrow and ten years from now. You tenderly call us to cast all our cares on you because you care for us—each one of us according to our particular circumstances, needs, weaknesses, and sufferings.

We rejoice that you are the Father of mercies and God of all comfort. What beautiful titles! Every kind word, expression of forgiveness, strengthening prayer, encouraging hug, act of service, and sympathetic tear comes from your great heart of mercy!

We thank you that you comfort us in all our affliction so we can comfort others in any affliction. Thank you that you never waste our pains. You use them to sanctify us and equip us to comfort others. How wonderful that you choose to use us to be your physician's assistants, to be the instruments of your loving-kindness, healing power, and encouragement. We give you praise for the glory of your grace in Jesus's name. Amen.

———

"**Lord, you were favorable to your land;** / you restored the fortunes of Jacob. / You forgave the iniquity of your people; / you covered all their sin. / You withdrew all your wrath; / you turned from your hot anger" (Ps. 85:1–3).

Heavenly Father, we glory in you for your stunning grace—we are amazed; we lift you up; we delight in you; we boast in you; we praise your name because you have shown us your favor—your undeserved kindness in Jesus Christ.

Instead of giving us what we deserved, you poured out on him your just wrath so you could withdraw it from us. By his work alone and for his glory alone you have forgiven all our sins and covered us with his righteousness. This is not abstract doctrine, Lord, but weighty and liberating reality!

Thank you for the security, peace, and hope your forgiveness and righteousness bring us, even on our worst days. Thank you that it is his performance, not ours, that makes us right with you. Thank you that it is his approval, not others', that satisfies our souls. Thank you that for our sakes you made him to be sin who knew no sin, so that in him we might become the righteousness of God.

Lord, we don't know what to make of this—we are not just righteous before you but we are your very righteousness! What freedom! What peace! What joy to be the righteousness of God in Christ! Amen.

———

"**For with you is the fountain of life;** / **in your light do we see light**" (Ps. 36:9).

Lord, we praise you for *the light of your creation* in the heavens: planets and stars, the light of the moon and the greater light of the sun, constellations and billions of spinning galaxies.

We thank you for *ten thousand reflections of your glory* on the earth: continents and oceans, meadows and grasslands, rivers and lakes, mountains and forests, waterfalls and wildflowers.

We gladly acknowledge *the greater light* imaged forth in human intellect, creativity, and resourcefulness—for people who excel in various trades, arts, education, governance, athletics, homemaking, farming, and various ministries. Truly Augustine was right when he praised the glory of God in the genius of man!

We glory in you for *the greatest light* of salvation in Christ (wonder upon wonder): his taking on humanity—not for thirty-three years but forever; his blameless life of holiness and love; his bearing all our griefs and sorrows, sicknesses and pains; his wrath-removing, curse-bearing, death-destroying, and Spirit-purchasing death; and his triumphant resurrection, which brought in a new age of everlasting righteousness and never-ending joy.

We thank you for the Spirit's present ministry of convicting us of sin, regenerating our hearts, illuminating your word, transforming our lives, equipping our ministries, and glorifying us with Christ when we see him face to face. We pray in Christ's name. Amen.

———

We give you thanks, Abba Father, with all our hearts and souls! Before the angels and saints in heaven we sing your praise! Before our families and friends, teachers and professors, celebrities and heroes, and this entire world we declare your surpassing glory. We praise you for your unfailing love and faithfulness toward us.

You have exalted above all things the majesty of your name and the authority of your word. All the princes and kings, presidents and prime ministers, and movers and shakers of this world will bow before you, for you rule over every place, person, tribe, and tongue forever.

We thank you, Father, that though you are high and lifted up and dwell in unapproachable light, you also care for the poor and needy, for those who are willing to humble themselves before you and seek your help. We are those needy people this morning, and we delight to come through Christ to exalt your glorious name. Amen.

———

Our heavenly Father through Jesus Christ, how can we adequately praise you for the gift of gifts—your own Son, begotten, not created; our Redeemer, representative, substitute, brother, and friend? His emptying himself of heavenly glory for our sake is incomprehensible; his measureless love for us is beyond our heart's grasp.

In Christ your Son we see a wonderful condescension. He came down to earth to raise us up to heaven, and he was made like us so we could become like him.

In Christ your Son we see amazing love. When we could not rise to him, he came down low to be near us and to draw us to himself.

In Christ your Son we see mighty power. When deity and humanity were infinitely apart, he united them in himself with indestructible unity, the uncreated and the created, the infinite and the finite.

In Christ your Son we see glorious wisdom. When we were utterly lost with no desire to return and no wisdom to plan our recovery, he became God-with-us to save us to the uttermost—as perfect man to shed his holy blood for us, to die a sinner's death in our place, to work out a perfect righteousness so we might be accepted.

Father, we stagger at the mystery of Christmas. We stumble for words to express your inexpressible glory, merciful kindness, and holy love. We thank you for the gift of Jesus who saves us from the guilt and shame, the power and misery of sin. We praise you for the one who is our shield, our glory, and the lifter of our heads. We worship you through him who is your perfect image, beloved Son, and delight of your heart.

Glory to you in the highest, Father! Together we praise you for your astounding, radical, costly, free, triumphant, glorious, redeeming love in Christ Jesus our Lord. Even in our wildest and best dreams we could never have imagined such an amazing salvation. We give you our hearts and our praise in the name of your beloved Son. Amen.

9

Prayers of Confession

HEAVENLY FATHER, how amazing we can address you as our Abba Father, all because of Jesus, who was descended from the royal line of David and declared to be your Son by his glorious resurrection from the dead. We thank you that you have saved us from the guilt and power of our sins by his death but confess that we still struggle with our sinful nature and often fall short of your glory.

We confess that the root of all our sin is that we still resist the truth of your authority and holiness because we want to do what is right in our own eyes.

We confess that we often exchange the truth of your infinite glory for degrading lies and worship and serve anything and everything but you.

We confess that our hearts often overflow with lust, envy, conflict, deceit, gossip, rebellion, pride, disobedience, and selfishness.

We confess that we are often foolish, faithless, heartless, and ruthless.

We confess that those who practice such things deserve to die.

Hear us now as we silently confess our sins to you. (Silent prayers of confession.)

Lord, how we praise you for the gospel of your Son, the power of God to save us from the uttermost of sin and misery to the uttermost of forgiveness and new life! We cry out with the psalmist: "The LORD is my strength and my song; / he has become my salvation. . . . / I shall not die, but I shall live, / and recount the deeds of the LORD" (Ps. 118:14, 17). In Jesus's name. Amen.

———

Lord, we just sang your praises and declared that you are the great joy of our lives. And that is our desire. But we confess that is often not the way we live. John said, "Do not love the world or the things in the world" (1 John 2:15). Jesus himself said, "Do not be anxious about your life . . . but seek first the kingdom of God and his righteousness" and all that you need will be added to you (Matt. 6:25, 33). We confess this morning that instead of seeking first your kingdom, we often seek first:

Our own provisions: We love what feels good, looks good, and gives us status. We dishonor you by fretting and worrying instead of trusting your affectionate sovereignty and praying for our daily bread.

Our own power: We want to manipulate others instead of honoring and serving them. We say we want America to be great, or our state, or our university, or our family, but the truth is each one of us wants to be great ourselves; each of us wants to be God.

Our own protection: We want to minimize all risk so we can hold on to the good lives we have and attain heaven on earth. So we panic or lash out when our earthly treasures are threatened.

Have mercy on us, Lord, as we silently confess our sins to you. (Silent prayers of confession.)

We thank you for your grace and mercy in Christ, Lord, and we ask that you would teach us to be like Jesus. May we live by every word that comes from your mouth, worship and serve you alone, and trust you instead of testing you.

We pray this in Jesus's name. Amen.

———

Father of mercies and God of all comfort, your word says that none is righteous, no, not one; no one understands or seeks after you. Each one of us has turned aside and devalued the worth of your holy image. We did this by nature before we knew your grace in Christ, and we still struggle against the weight of pride and unbelief.

We know that your perfect law brings every one of us to you this morning convicted of our sins, speechless before you, and accountable to your majesty.

We confess our many and grievous sins. We confess as a nation, as your people at URC, and as individuals that we love prosperity more than being poor in spirit, our rights more than our responsibilities, factions more than unity, superiority more than humility, autonomy more than dependence, pleasure more than sacrifice, tolerance more than righteousness, nationalism more than the kingdom of God, materialism more than spiritual blessings, and power more than service.

Hear us now as we silently confess our sins to you. (Silent prayers of confession.)

"But now the righteousness of God has been manifested apart from the law, although the Law and the Prophets bear witness to it—the righteousness of God through faith in Jesus Christ for all who believe. For there is no distinction: for all have sinned and fall short of the glory of God, and are justified by his grace as a gift, through the redemption that is in Christ Jesus" (Rom. 3:21–24).

Thanks be to God through our Lord Jesus Christ!

———

Our Lord and God, your word tells us that if we say we have no sin, we deceive ourselves and the truth is not in us. So we confess this morning that we still too often live according to the flesh and not the Spirit.

We covet what others have or have achieved; we hate not only our enemies but sometimes even our own friends and family; we envy because we do not believe you are wise and good; we stir up strife and conflict because we want what we want when we want it. We are often idolaters and adulterers, friends of the world and in rebellion against you, Lord.

We confess that we gossip but call it sharing, we slander but call it honesty, we boast but call it self-confidence. We are often indifferent to sin and call it worldly wisdom and tolerance.

We do not hate what is evil or hold fast to what is good; we do not outdo one another in showing honor. We are not fervent in spirit as we serve you.

Have mercy on us miserable offenders, Father, not because we deserve it but because Jesus has lived our life and died our death. Forgive our many sins and change our hearts and lives through the gospel. We pray in his holy name. Amen.

———

Father, in the light of your goodness and glory, we confess our many sins. All our sins flow from hearts that so easily rebel against your will and exchange your infinite beauty for corrupted images.

We drink from the polluted streams of sin instead of the living waters of righteousness. As a result we refuse contentment in you and crave what others have; we refuse humble service and jealously attack one another; we refuse looking to the interests of others and fight to get our way; we refuse liberating worship and become slaves to god substitutes.

Have mercy on us, O God, for our foolishness, faithlessness, and pride. Hear us now as we silently confess our sins to you. (Silent prayers of confession.)

Thank you, Father, that although we have sinned against you in thought, word, and deed, there is now no condemnation for those who are in Christ Jesus. Thanks be to God for his indescribable gift!

———

Lord, we thank you for your Son, the light of the world, who has brought the light of the gospel into our lives. And although it's sometimes painful, we thank you that this gospel light also illuminates our sin so we can confess and receive your forgiveness.

In these few days before Christmas we confess that we often act more like blind men than wise men. We pursue comfort, pleasure, success, and self-esteem more than righteousness, godliness, faith, and love. Our relationships are often marked by clueless indifference, hidden agendas, and silent resentment. Our devotion to you is distracted and half-hearted while our devotion to ourselves is razor-sharp and intense.

These sins are demeaning to you and deadly to us. Have mercy on us, gracious Father. Forgive us, cleanse us, raise us up, free us, and fill us with genuine love for you and our neighbor.

Thank you that, as the psalmist says, with you there is forgiveness, steadfast love, and plentiful redemption for all who come humbly in Jesus's name (Ps. 130). Amen.

———

Our great God and Father, we praise you for your generous gifts but acknowledge that you are the best gift of all. Your love is better than life, and in your presence there is fullness of joy. Surely our cup of blessings is full and our cup of thanksgiving should overflow.

But Lord, we confess that this is often not true. How quick we are to forget your mercies, neglect your graces, and disobey your commands. How easily and naturally we take your good gifts of material comforts, loved ones, jobs, accomplishments, and personal plans and turn them into heartbreaking and soul-destroying idols. We pray "your kingdom come and your will be done," but then ruthlessly pursue our own agendas. Instead of sacrificing ourselves for the good of others, we manipulate, control, and punish even those we love the most.

Have mercy on us, Lord, for the sake of your Son, who died to forgive our sins and to free us from living for ourselves, so we could find our greatest happiness in your glory and others' good. Amen.

———

Lord, you have called us to be your witnesses: to live holy lives and to boldly tell the good news of salvation in Jesus Christ. We confess that we have failed to do this, often miserably.

We have taken your salvation for granted, forgetting the blood-stained agony of Christ in the garden, the anguished cry from the cross, and the triumphant resurrection from the dead.

We have treated your forgiveness as a light and inconsequential thing. We have felt entitled to your tender mercy and have despised your discipline.

We have chosen to stay in the darkness of our sin when the sun of righteousness has risen with healing in his wings.

We have been too concerned about our childish pleasures and fragile egos to live out and give away the radiant joy of knowing Christ.

We have been witnesses to our own selfish agendas and petty kingdoms rather than to your glorious purpose to unite and restore all things in the kingdom of your Son.

Forgive what we have been, Lord, and make us like your Son so that the whole earth is full of your glory and every knee bows to the King of ages. In his name we pray. Amen.

———

Abba, Father, even as we worship you, we are painfully aware of all the ways we fall short of your glory. Instead of declaring your steadfast love in the morning and your faithfulness by night, we frantically scramble around trying to make sense of our day all on our own and finally fall exhausted into bed without acknowledging your presence or calling on your help. Forgive us, O Lord.

Instead of being made glad by your work of creation and redemption, we often rejoice in the works of our own hands or those of others—we confess we love Facebook, college sports, family, vacations, food, comfort, success, and self-image more than we love you. Forgive us, O Lord.

Instead of singing for joy to you, we go through the motions of quiet times, growth groups, and Sunday services without the trembling joy that comes from really knowing you, the living God. Forgive us, O Lord.

Forgive the distorted image of you we present to the world, forgive the commands we neglect or disobey, and forgive the god substitutes we worship. Have mercy on us, O Lord, for your great name's sake! Amen.

———

Lord, we thank you that we are redeemed sinners, but we have sinned in this last week in many ways. We think ourselves faithful believers, when in fact our affection for you is weak and fickle. We imagine ourselves humble servants as we manipulate others to get what we want. We entertain condemning thoughts toward others in our hearts even though Jesus has taken our condemnation upon himself. We take your name in vain as we speak passionately about you but deny you by the way we live. We are easily led astray by the seduction of sex, control, possessions, approval, and various self-justifying schemes. Have mercy on us!

We are sinners indeed, Lord, but by your grace we are redeemed. We confess with joy that Jesus was condemned so we could be forgiven and counted righteous. Jesus was cursed so we could be blessed. Jesus was rejected so we could be welcomed. Jesus was made sin so we could be made the righteousness of God. Jesus died so we could be raised to imperishable life.

Such love! Such mercy! Such justice! Such wisdom! Praise the Lord, O my soul!

———

Father, we know that we please you the most when we are most pleased with your Son, our mediator, King, and brother. We adore him as the radiance of your glory and the exact imprint of your nature.

But Lord, we would be liars if we didn't admit that our sin often blinds us to the glory of Jesus. The lesser lights of worldly pleasures, people-pleasing, and living comfortably outshine him in our hearts.

We confess our vanity, foolishness, cowardice, and rebellion as unfitting for your people.

We thank you for your mercy, patience, forgiveness, and power to renew us in love and obedience. Open our eyes again to the sun of righteousness, the star of Jacob, the light of the world.

Captivate us with his beauty, liberate us with his grace, and motivate us with his love so that once again we live lives of grateful worship and service. In Jesus's name. Amen.

———

Our God and Father, you have encouraged us to confess our sins to you, assuring us that you are faithful to forgive and cleanse us from all unrighteousness.

In that assurance we confess that we often have other gods before you. We take refuge in and serve and live for created things rather than the Creator, who is forever blessed. Forgive us for preferring others' company to yours, for escaping through various creature comforts rather than taking refuge in you, for yawning through Sunday worship, and for half-hearted obedience. These are serious sins.

As we indulge in this idolatry, we break many other commandments as well. We worship according to our distorted images of you. We speak your name without true understanding or reverence. We break your Sabbath by not resting and rejoicing in Christ's finished work and by being indifferent to the needs of others. We dishonor our parents by disobedience or disrespect. We harbor bitterness in our hearts. We sin sexually in thought and deed. We steal possessions or reputations from others. We exaggerate and lie. We turn innocent desires into dangerous cravings.

Have mercy on us, O God, for Jesus's sake. Amen.

———

O great God of heaven, we come to you now in the name of Jesus our Savior. We confess that our enemies, the world, the flesh, and the devil, have battled against our souls this week and have gotten the better of us more often than we want to admit.

We confess that the world has seduced us with tinsel treasures that we can see and feel and taste and touch and that promise immediate comfort and status—and we have betrayed you, the Lord and lover of our souls. *Have mercy on us.*

We confess that our own sinful nature is, as C. S. Lewis said, a zoo of lusts and has led us to fret and demand and retaliate and to seek our own glory—even when these things leave us empty and ashamed. *Have mercy on us.*

We confess that the enemy of our souls has lied and we have been deceived; he has accused and we have cowered; he has put the hook in our mouth and we have bitten. We have turned traitor again and again. *Have mercy on us.*

We confess that in all these things we have broken your laws, dishonored your name, rebelled against your authority, and despised your love. We are weak and wounded, sick and sore because of our sins and miseries. *Have mercy on us.*

Let's confess the sins of our hearts and lives silently before the Lord. (Silent prayers of confession.)

Thank you that there is abundant forgiveness through the blood of the cross when we confess our sins.

Lord, teach us your truth in Jesus so that we might be free. Remember your mercy in Jesus and not our sins, and we will praise your goodness. Meet us in our trials and troubles, and we will walk in obedience. In Jesus's name we pray. Amen.

———

Our Father in heaven, we confess that we often walk blindly through this world of glory distracted and blinded by our lusts and fears.

We don't give you thanks and praise because we're turned in on ourselves.

We don't submit to your kingly authority because we love our own agenda and will.

We don't tremble before your word and we disregard your commandments because we are seeking our own righteousness and kingdom instead of yours.

We don't reflect your holiness and are often enslaved to our petty concerns, irritable attitudes, and loveless ways.

Forgive us, Father, for loving ourselves more than you and our neighbors, for falling desperately short of your glory, and for breaking your good commands.

Pause and pray silently. (Silent prayers of confession.)

Hear this word of assurance from Psalm 130:7–8: "O Israel, hope in the LORD! / For with the LORD there is steadfast love, and with him is plentiful redemption. / And he will redeem Israel / from all his iniquities." Amen.

———

In the light of your blazing holiness, Lord, we see and confess our many sins.

We treat you as if you merely have a supporting role in the story of our self-fulfillment.

We value your gifts of health and wealth, comfort and security, success and accomplishment more than we value your infinite glory.

We profess faith in Christ and then live as practical atheists: leaning on our own understanding, trying to save ourselves through our own performance, and judging others in a way we would never want to be judged.

We live as tourists instead of ambassadors in our culture, buying up trinkets for ourselves instead of giving our lives away to others.

We indulge lusts of sexual sin, material greed, selfish resentment, and self-punishment, and then try to hide them from you and others.

Forgive our sins, Lord. Heal our remaining corruption. Set us free to serve and witness to Christ in the power of the Holy Spirit.

Thank you that in Christ there is no condemnation and that the law of the Spirit of life has set us free from the law of sin and death. Amen.

———

Abba, Father, we confess to you today that we are slow to understand and appreciate the gospel of your grace. So often we are rebellious and resistant to change into the image of Christ.

We sin in countless ways, but always because we prefer countless things to your beloved Son and then live in ways that belittle his glory and dishonor your name.

Forgive us for treasuring friends and family, jobs and possessions, popularity and comfort more than the praise of your glory.

Forgive us for self-serving cowardice when you have called us to loving courage in witness and service.

Forgive us for pursuing the American dream more than the kingdom of God.

As the old prayer says, we are miserable offenders and can plead only your amazing grace, your righteousness in Christ, your salvation through the cross, and your transforming power through the Spirit.

Thank you for your gospel promise that everyone who calls upon the name of the Lord will be saved. In Jesus's name. Amen.

O Father, how often we are weary of our sins and sufferings. How often we grieve the feebleness of our faith, the wavering of our hope, and stinginess of our love. How often we look at our lives, families, neighborhoods, city, and beyond, and see only foolishness, futility, and frustration. We sorrow over the conflict between various groups and races, the corruption that pollutes and degrades our sexuality, and the callousness to your holiness. We see these everywhere.

We are especially grieved because of the heinous sin of one man and the mishandling of many in authority that has devastated hundreds of young women and their families and rocked our community. And we acknowledge that it is not just those involved in this evil that need your mercy and grace, but we ourselves.

Father, as you have shown grace and favor in the past, will you restore us again and make us whole? Revive us again and cause us to rejoice in you. Lift up Jesus to us and then send us to lift him up to neighbors and nations! Proclaim Jesus to us and move us to proclaim him to others! Counsel Jesus to us and make us instruments of the Wonderful Counselor!

Grant us your salvation from the crippling guilt and paralyzing shame and enslaving power of our sins. Strengthen us to know the height and depth and breadth and length of your holy love, and then enable us to sacrificially love those you have brought into our lives.

We pray this confidently in Jesus's name. Amen.

Our Lord and God, as we thank and praise you for your great goodness to us, we confess that we have sinned grievously this week in thought, word, and deed.

We have often broken the first great commandment to love you with all our heart, soul, mind, and strength. Instead of being faithful to you, we have given our hearts to anything and everything but you—jobs and careers, hobbies and entertainment, friends and family, small comforts and trivial successes—all of these mere shadows of your all-surpassing glory.

In breaking the first commandment we have inevitably broken the second: we have treated others as obstacles to avoid or pawns to manipulate to get our own way and serve our own purposes.

Hear us now as we silently confess our sins to you. (Silent prayers of confession.)

Forgive us for the sake of your great name. Make us clean through the blood of Christ. Give us new life through the Spirit. And write your law on our hearts so that we walk in holiness and love this week. In the name of our heavenly Father, our Savior Jesus, and the Holy Spirit we pray. Amen.

"The sorrows of those who run after another god shall multiply"
(Ps. 16:4).

Lord God, this is a clear and merciful warning: those who serve god substitutes bring dishonor to you and sorrow to themselves. We are sorry and ashamed to admit that this often describes us. You are more generous and kind than our wildest imaginations, and yet we so easily go astray in our hearts.

You offer us Christ himself and every spiritual blessing in him. You offer us wisdom, protection, provision, and abundance. You offer us the way of life, fullness of joy, and pleasures forevermore.

But we confess to our shame that our hearts are prone to wander, chasing gods of achievement, approval, image, pleasure, control, and a thousand other things. How foolish, how unfaithful, how crooked we are.

Have mercy on us, Lord. Remember that we are dust, and show compassion on those who fear you. Forgive the sins we now confess silently to you. (Silent prayers of confession.)

Father, we are so thankful that you are good. You love to forgive all our iniquities because Jesus became sin for us, heal all our diseases because you made him sick for us, redeem our lives from the pit because Jesus became a curse for us, crown us with steadfast love and mercy because Jesus was crowned with thorns for us, and satisfy us with good because Jesus cried out in thirst for us.

Bless the Lord, O my soul, and forget not all his benefits in Christ! Bless the Lord! In Jesus's name. Amen.

10

Prayers of Supplication

"OFFER TO GOD A SACRIFICE of thanksgiving, / and perform your vows to the Most High, / and call upon me in the day of trouble; / I will deliver you, and you shall glorify me" (Ps. 50:14–15).

In the confidence of this precious promise, Father, we bring to you our many needs. For some this is truly a day of trouble, and so we call on your name and ask you to deliver us.

We pray for our pastoral and ministry staff, for our church officers and leaders. Give them wisdom to serve wisely and well in this time of disruption of normal activities. Ministry is a great privilege and joy, but there are weights and burdens as well. *O Lord, deliver us and empower these ministries by your Spirit.*

We pray for those who are physically weak or sick. Our bodies are often frail, sickness abounds, and we depend on you for every breath. *O Lord, deliver us and restore to health those who are ill.*

We pray for those who struggle with anxiety or depression, loneliness or grief. There are ten thousand heartaches in this life, and they press many down with a heavy weight. *O Lord, deliver us and bring tender mercies and renewing grace to those weighed down.*

We pray for those who deal with unwanted singleness, painful marriages, childlessness, hurting or wayward children. *O Lord, deliver us and bring comfort and confidence of your good purposes to those whose longings are unfulfilled.*

We pray for ourselves—for single-mindedness and undivided hearts. We pray for holy affections and righteous lives. We confess that we are often weak before our enemies of the world, the flesh, and the devil. We stumble and fall through unbelief, pride, and wayward hearts. *O Lord, deliver us and cause us to walk in a way that is pleasing to you.*

We pray for our country during this election year. Politics is so often contentious and contemptuous. *O Lord, deliver us and give us leaders better than we deserve who will seek your wisdom to govern well.*

We pray for individuals, universities, cities, and nations affected by the coronavirus. This has caused great disruption and fear for many. We look to you, our heavenly Father, always reigning in wisdom, power, and love. We pray for clear minds and steady hearts for those who govern, for those who seek a cure, and for each one of us. We pray for wisdom to take proper precautions and faith to reach out to the lost and needy. This is a painful but merciful reminder that we are not in control of our lives and that you can call any of us at any time into your holy presence. Give us wisdom to number our days and to make the best use of our time, for the days are evil. *O Lord, deliver us, bring many people to Christ through this, and then please bring a quick end to this pandemic.*

We pray finally for fruitful gospel ministry throughout the world. We pray for our own missionaries and all who bring good news to the world. Again, those who witness in the name of Christ will face many hardships. *O Lord, deliver us and work powerfully through your word to save your elect.*

All these things we pray with gratitude and confidence in Jesus's name. Amen.

———

Father, you know each one of us intimately, and you know our weaknesses. We are vulnerable to assaults on our bodies and souls, marriages and families, friendships and acquaintances, work and ministry, purposes and plans, thoughts and emotions. Like Paul, we often feel afflicted in every way, perplexed, persecuted, and struck down. How we thank you that Jesus our Lord has taken upon himself our own humanity and vulnerability to these assaults. Thank you that he earned our righteousness by his perfect obedience, removed our sins by his death, and raised us to indestructible life by his resurrection. Thank you that because he suffered when he was tempted, he is able to help us when we are tempted and afflicted.

Father, Jesus taught us to pray that you would keep us from trials and temptations that would overwhelm and destroy us. So we ask that you would be with all of us (church staff and leaders, marriages and families, singles of all ages), protect us, rescue us, strengthen us, and deliver us safe to your eternal glory and joy. Teach us daily to pray that we not enter into temptation, and teach us to put on the full armor of God.

May the belt of the truth of Jesus set us free from the lies, accusations, and condemnation that continually beset us.

May the breastplate of Christ's imputed and imparted righteousness guard our hearts from the desires of our flesh, the desires of our eyes, and the pride of life.

May the gospel of Christ's peace and wholeness make us ready and eager to bring good news to others.

May the shield of faith in Christ extinguish all the flaming darts of doubt, fear, and lust that come from the evil one.

May the helmet of Christ's salvation fill our minds with the joy of our salvation.

May we wield the sword of the Spirit effectively and live by every word that comes from the mouth of God.

We praise you, Father, that Jesus is our shield, our glory, and the lifter of our heads. We thank you for your precious promises in Psalm 91:

> Because he holds fast to me in love, I will deliver him;
>   I will protect him, because he knows my name.
> When he calls to me, I will answer him;
>   I will be with him in trouble;
>   I will rescue him and honor him.
> With long life I will satisfy him
>   and show him my salvation. (Ps. 91:14–16)

We pray this all with thanksgiving. Amen.

———

Thank you, Father, that you have begun a good work in us and will bring it to completion in the day of Christ Jesus. But Lord, you know that we are not home yet; this world, our individual worlds, are still subject to great brokenness and frustration. And even we who have the Spirit still groan inwardly as we wait for the dawn of salvation to become the full day of salvation. And so, Lord, we eagerly lift up our needs and requests to you. This morning we pray for:

Those whose chronic loneliness becomes acutely painful during this Christmas season and for those who have lost loved ones and grieve their absence. *Lord Jesus, would you be their comfort.*

Those whose marriages are estranged and who have lost hope of any real intimacy. *Lord Jesus, would you be their peace.*

For those who ache to be married and see no realistic prospect. *Lord Jesus, would you be the lover of their souls.*

For those struggling with acute or chronic illness. *Lord Jesus, would you be their healer.*

For those unemployed or underemployed or those whose jobs are a daily battle with demands and discouragement. *Lord, Jesus, would you be their reward.*

For those who struggle to have even a mustard seed of faith, who lack assurance and live under a cloud of condemnation every day. *Lord Jesus, would you be their sun of righteousness.*

For those who are victims of natural disasters and destruction, hunger and poverty, racism and oppression, war and terrorism. *Lord Jesus, would you be their restoration.*

We think especially of our brothers and sisters across the world who are hated and who hurt in various ways because of their faith in Jesus. *Lord Jesus, would you be their glory.*

In all these circumstances and in countless more, Lord, help us remember that there is now no condemnation in Christ Jesus and there will never be any separation from his love. Continue to guard us through faith, call us each by name, cause us to walk in a manner pleasing to you, and give us a strong and steady hope for that day when all sorrow and sighing will flee away and everlasting joy will be upon our heads in your glad presence. We pray in hope through Christ our Lord. Amen.

———

Heavenly Father, we pray that you would revive us in your grace. We confess that we get blind and dull and weary. Impassion us and empower us to bring the gospel of salvation to all people: people in our own neighborhoods, workplaces, dorms, and schools, and to people all over the world who have not yet heard of your grace in Christ, the only mediator between God and man.

Bless every ministry here at University Reformed Church: pastors and staff, growth groups and Bible studies, men's and women's ministries, shepherding and mercy ministries, and all evangelism, discipleship, and mission ministries.

Lord, may your grace heal all who are sick, strengthen all who are weak and wavering in their faith, convict all who are unconverted or drifting, and encourage all who are weighed down with burdens of body and soul. Strengthen marriages, encourage singles, train children, sustain the aging, and sanctify us all.

By your grace, would you expose and tear down the idolatrous altars of materialism, narcissism, racism, and terrorism in our country. Bring peace to our neighborhoods, justice to our courts, truth to our schools, integrity to our government, reconciliation between races, and most of all, the gospel to every tribe and tongue.

And finally, Lord, with John Newton we say,

Thro' many dangers, toils, and snares, I have already come;
'tis grace has brought me safe thus far, and grace will lead
me home.[1]

Amen.

———

Father, in the light of your glorious gospel, we lift up our petitions to you.

We pray that you will bring Holy Spirit revival to University Reformed Church. Give us such head and heart knowledge of your salvation that we see and repent of our idolatries of comfortable materialism, selfish control, corrupting pleasures, and soul-dulling entertainments.

Help us to no longer live for our idolatrous kingdoms. Rather, intoxicate us with the surpassing beauty and greatness of Jesus Christ. Teach us to eat and drink and watch basketball and go out with friends and raise families and go to work and be intimate with our spouses and lead small groups and study and play and read the Bible all for the glory of your Son.

Pour out your tender mercies on those in our midst and community who are suffering terribly: those who have lost children or can't have them or don't know what to do with them; those who are in struggling marriages or desperately wishing they were married; those who have aging spouses or parents who need more care than they can give them; those who need a job or hate the ones they have; those who so much want to be free from bad attitudes

1   "Amazing Grace," 1779.

and habits and have all but given up hope; those who are spiritually lost or confused or just indifferent. Have mercy on us, Lord.

Where sin and suffering run rampant in the world, make your
grace run higher, longer, wider, and deeper. We think of those
suffering from natural disasters in Haiti and other places, those
persecuted for their faith in North Korea, China, Iraq, and many
other nations, those who lack basic necessities of life, those suffering from the terrors and devastation of war, and those blinded
by false religion and worldly values and the deceitfulness of their
own hearts. Have mercy on them all in Jesus's name. Amen.

**Lord, the whole world groans in the anguish of frustration,
decay, corruption, and death.** Have mercy on a world in darkness.

Revive us and set us free to pray, give, mobilize, send, and go
to the hard places across the world. Make us Jesus's ambassadors
of faith, hope, and love.

Because of your tender mercy, you have given your own Son
to give light to those in darkness and to guide the world into the
way of peace. So make us the kind of people who would rather
use our time and resources to be part of your glorious plan of
salvation than to use them merely to become more enslaved to
trivial pursuits.

May your gospel go deep and wide in our hearts and far and
wide in the world so that Jesus Christ may be all and in all to
your everlasting praise and glory. Amen.

We come to your throne of grace, Lord, where we not only receive mercy for our failures but grace to help us in time of need.

We pray for healthy marriages that show to the world the magnificent sacrifice of Christ and the glad submission of the church.

We pray for children who, because they have been brought up in the discipline, instruction, and affection of the Lord, honor their parents and live long and happy and fruitful lives.

We pray for our leaders at University Reformed Church—staff, elders, deacons, deaconesses, teachers, missionaries, and many others—that they might be enabled to serve lovingly, skillfully, and joyfully. Grant vision, leadership, integrity, resources, and gifts to fulfill their callings.

We pray also for our community—that you would bless and prosper colleges and universities, state government, private and public schools, and the many businesses in the greater Lansing area. We pray for peace and righteousness in our city, state, and country so that we can lead quiet lives and spread the good news that there is one mediator between God and man, one Savior of sinners, and one Lord over all.

We ask that you would strengthen and comfort those who are suffering in the world—our persecuted brothers and sisters as well as those whose lives have been devastated by natural disasters, wars, and various oppressions, whether racial, economic, political, or religious.

And most of all, we pray, come quickly, Lord Jesus. Only you can make this broken world whole again. We do not put our trust in princes or presidents, in chariots or modern armies, in technology or medical breakthroughs, in pop psychology or world religions. We trust in you alone. Come, Lord Jesus, and bring the completion of our salvation and the consummation of all we long for. Amen.

———

Lord, we thank you that when you call us to faith in Christ, you call us into a body of believers, a family of God. We know that we worship today in a worldwide fellowship of your people all over the world. Some, like us, enjoy relative peace and prosperity, others, actually the majority of Christians, experience great suffering and need. Paul says that if one member suffers, all suffer together.

So this morning we come in solidarity with our suffering brothers and sisters, to offer up prayers for them: to thank you for their faithfulness and to pray for their healing, hope, and perseverance. We are commanded in Hebrews to "remember those who are in prison, as though in prison with them, and those who are mistreated, since [we] also are in the body" (13:3). Lord, we confess that we disobey this command continually; in fact, we probably seldom even think of it.

Lord, we ask first of all that you would forgive our forgetfulness, indifference, and complacency toward our suffering brothers and sisters. How often do we make any attempt to learn about the suffering church and to pray for them? We thank you for the blood of Christ that cleanses us from this sin of indifference, as well as all our other sins.

And now we do take a stand beside them in the Spirit to lift them up to your compassion, grace, and power. We pray for Uzbekistan, Iran, Pakistan, Egypt, and all over Asia.

For all our suffering brothers and sisters we pray that you would provide the means of grace: Bibles; the presence and power of the Holy Spirit; people to visit them; food, clothing, shelter, and medical help. We pray that you would give them grace to forgive their tormentors as they have been forgiven by you. We pray that this grace would be a powerful witness to unbelievers and many would come to Christ as a result of their witness. We ask that you would comfort those separated from loved ones, marginalized, oppressed, raped, and tortured. We pray that you would raise up advocates for them in positions of authority. We pray that they would count everything as loss because of the surpassing worth of knowing Christ, that they would learn the secret of contentment in any and every circumstance, and that Christ would be honored in their bodies, whether by life or by death.

All these things we pray in confidence in Jesus's name. Amen.

———

Lord we thank you for the country we live in. You have blessed us with many freedoms and much prosperity. And yet these don't evidence your approval or ensure our future—you alone decide the fate of nations and governments. We pray for our president and his administration, for Congress and all legislators, for all our courts high and low. Please give these men and women your understanding and righteousness to make good decisions and just laws and wise rulings.

We pray that you would reveal your righteousness by reviving your people to preach the gospel, speak out for the unborn, declare the truth, care for the widow and orphan, and keep ourselves unstained from the world.

We pray for missionaries in hard places—in Africa, the Middle East, Asia, Europe, and the Americas—for protection and provision to preach the gospel and make disciples of all nations.

We pray for the peace of our own city of Lansing: for businesses and state government and neighborhoods and families to thrive. We pray for safety in schools and on the streets and in homes. We pray for area churches to preach the gospel humbly but boldly and to do all manner of good works so that many residents of Lansing will see and glorify the Father.

Finally, we pray that Jesus will come soon. No political party or educational system or modern technology or anything else can bring in the kingdom of God—that belongs to the Lord Jesus Christ. We pray for the day when he will subdue all God's enemies and submit himself and all things to the Father, who is all in all. Even so, come, Lord Jesus! Amen.

———

Lord, we rejoice that you invite us to make our requests known to you with thanksgiving and so we offer these petitions.

We pray for our elders. Thank you for calling them through your Spirit and church to this office of spiritual leadership. We ask for a sense of urgency and wise shepherding as well as the grace to serve in word and prayer and oversight. Ezekiel 34 says they are to strengthen the weak, heal the sick, bind up the injured, bring back those straying, shepherd the flock, and exercise oversight. Lord, no one is sufficient for these things, but you are their sufficiency and wisdom and righteousness.

We pray for our diaconate. Thank you for calling them to this office of mercy and help. The personal, health, financial, and other practical needs of our congregation are often complex. Give them tender hearts and clear minds as they minister in Jesus's name. Help them to make it a glad thing for people to receive help here. Give them endurance and patience with joy as they serve the church at University Reformed Church. Let the works of Christ's mercy abound here so people see his beauty and give you glory.

Finally, and most importantly, we pray for gospel revival for our lives and church and throughout the whole world. May Christ be lifted up in the power of the Spirit. May countless men and women, boys and girls be brought to repentance and faith. May all true Christians be unified in one body, one Spirit, one hope, one Lord, one faith, one baptism, one God and Father of all. May you cause us to persevere and grow in holiness, joy, and fruitful witness. And may you speed the day when you will wipe away every tear and death shall be no more, neither shall there be mourning nor crying nor pain anymore. We pray in Jesus's name. Amen.

———

Heavenly Father, as we move into the Thanksgiving and Christmas season, we are aware of those who are in great need.

For those in our congregation who are grieving the loss of loved ones or the loss of employment or the loss of health or the loss of hope, we pray your deep comfort.

For the poor and homeless in Lansing, we pray your practical mercies. Empower your churches, and the Lansing Rescue

Mission, and other Christian ministries to humbly and gladly reach out to the needy with words and works that bring life.

For those throughout the world who suffer unspeakably—for those in the Philippines who need food and clothing and shelter and medicine; for your persecuted church who need to be filled with your power to endure with joy; for those in war-torn places who need peace; for all those lost in sin who need a Savior, we pray that you would be the Father of mercies and the God of all comfort.

We ask, Father, that all who walk in the darkness of sin and suffering would see a great light! May the cry of millions this year be, "For to us a child is born, / to us a son is given; / and the government shall be upon his shoulder, / and his name shall be called / Wonderful Counselor, Mighty God, / Everlasting Father, Prince of Peace" (Isa. 9:6).

We pray this to your everlasting praise, Father, in Jesus's name. Amen!

———

Gracious God and Father, we bring to you our petitions, thankful that you delight to give good gifts to those who ask in Jesus's name.

We pray for grace to be poured out on our church staff and leaders: pastoral, ministry, and support staff; elders, deacons, and deaconesses; growth group leaders, teachers of children, youth, and adults. Do a great gospel work here, bringing people to faith, discipling them, and training them for service. Grant us every resource to carry out these ministries and cause us to overflow with joy, praise, and service.

Give hope to those who are discouraged relationally, financially, or emotionally. Heal those who are ill. Comfort those who are grieving, and grant renewed passion to those who are apathetic.

We pray for marriages to be strong, families to be united, and singles to believe that they are essential to our church and have valuable gifts to offer.

We pray for spiritual renewal in our city. Pour out your Spirit on your children here at University Reformed Church and in every gospel-loving church in our area. May we know and love and teach the meaning of redemption: that you have delivered us from the guilt and power of sin through the cross and are transforming us through your Spirit.

We pray for our nation, that you would turn the hearts of our leaders from idolatrous ideologies and selfish ambition to righteousness and compassion. Turn the hearts of our neighbors from deadly desires and false refuges to fullness of joy and eternal security.

We pray for the world. We pray for troubled places where there is conflict and persecution of our brothers and sisters: Iran, Egypt, Pakistan, Uganda, Syria, and others. Strengthen the suffering church with endurance and power through the Spirit so that Christ would dwell in their hearts and that they would be faithful and fruitful witnesses for him.

Finally, we pray for all missionaries, that you would give them protection, passion, and power to bring the gospel to all nations, especially to the unreached people groups. Give them grace to both get the gospel right and get the gospel out. May the name of Jesus be exalted by word and deed in every land, and may many lost sheep come home to the Father. May your glory, triune God, be over all the earth and your name be praised forever. Amen.

———

"For we do not want you to be unaware, brothers, of the afflic-tion we experienced. . . . For we were so utterly burdened beyond our strength that we despaired of life itself" (2 Cor. 1:8).

Gracious Father, we confess that our lives seem often unbearably hard: too many bills to pay and not enough money; heartbreaking grief over the loss of a loved one or cherished dream; distant or hostile relationships—sometimes within our own families; bad health and frightening medical reports; disabled or wayward or suffering children; overpowering emotions and unruly thoughts; Job-like assaults when we thought we were walking close to you.

We lament a divided country where fear and confusion and oppression seem to be winning. Lord, how can we bear living in such a sinful and broken world? Yet we take comfort from the fact that you sent your Son into the heart of darkness of this world to live the life we couldn't; to die the death we deserved; to rise to make us new creations; to ascend to the highest place of rule and intercession; and to come again to make every wrong thing right. We thank you that because of his incarnation he gets it; he sympathizes; he understands our temptations to cringe in fear or lash out in anger or escape into false refuges. We now draw near in the name of the one who was tempted in every way we are, yet without sin. How we need Jesus; how we need him to give rest and peace to our weary souls and hurting bodies.

Teach us, Lord, to accept that we are only jars of clay but that the surpassing power belongs to you; that although we are afflicted, perplexed, persecuted, and struck down by the sins and sufferings of life, we are *not* crushed, driven to despair, forsaken, or destroyed. We may feel like we are barely making it today, but your resurrection power is sustaining us. Thank you, Lord! Teach us to put on the full armor of God that we might face the evil day or week or month or year and be found still standing. Help us to see that when life feels like a living death, we are actually being called to carry in our bodies the death of Jesus so that his life will be seen in our mortal flesh. Help us to be encouraged that when death is at work in us, we are actually bringing life to others, sometimes by just suffering well. Remind us that the suffering of this week is only light and momentary compared to the eternal weight of glory that will be revealed to us. Help us to discipline ourselves to look to what is unseen and sometimes unfelt—your continual presence and the rock-solid promises of your word to work all things for our good. Grant to us the power of the Holy Spirit to help us to endure with joy, looking to the all-surpassing glory and joy that await us. Through Christ our Lord. Amen.

———

"First of all, then, I urge that supplications, prayers, intercessions, and thanksgivings be made for all people, for kings and all who are in high positions" (1 Tim. 2:1–2).

Lord, we pray for the leaders and citizens of our country: for our president and all governors and mayors and city councils, and for all lawmakers and judges at every level. There is no authority except that which comes from you, and so we pray for these men and women to look beyond their own opinions, beyond polls and conventional wisdom, beyond political correctness. Grant that they may look to you, to your wisdom and righteousness in order to make decisions that affect all of us. We pray for civility and reason to prevail in the presidential election and that you would guide the outcome according to your perfect wisdom. Save us from the blind leading the blind into ever more ungodliness and foolishness. You must lead us, O thou great Jehovah, for we truly are in a barren land.[2]

Lord, our heart's desire is not that we might make America great but your name great; not that we would continue to lead self-indulgent and self-satisfied lives but that we might lead peaceful and quiet lives, godly and dignified in every way. This glorifies you, satisfies us, and gives opportunities for the saving message of the gospel. In order that all people might come to the knowledge of the truth, we pray for safe neighborhoods where neighbors look out for one another and treat each other with respect. We pray for well-run schools where every student is free from physical and emotional harm, ungodly teaching, and politically correct nonsense. We pray for successful businesses where employees give a good day's work, employers treat and pay employees fairly, and helpful goods and services are provided to the community. And we pray for gospel-preaching churches where Christ is exalted, the Bible is taught, and disciples are made.

Finally, Lord, we make these intercessions with thanksgiving. We thank you for this wondrous creation that makes your glories known; for all the blessings of the gospel that reach as far as the curse is found; for one another, the "excellent ones" in

---

2   See William Williams, "Guide Me, O Thou Great Jehovah," 1745.

whom we truly do delight; and for food and drink and families and vacations and freedom and jobs and houses and a thousand other blessings that you have given us richly to enjoy. We believe and tremble that each of these blessings was purchased with the precious blood of Jesus.

"Not to us, O LORD, not to us, but to your name give glory, / for the sake of your steadfast love and your faithfulness!" (Ps. 115:1). Amen.

———

Father, we thank you that you invite us to come today with our needs and promise to give what is good when we ask in Jesus's name.

We ask that you would bless each of these precious new members. May each of them grow in "faith working though love" through the worship, fellowship, and accountability here at University Reformed Church. We pray for their marriages and families to thrive; for their work in and out of the home to be blessed; for opportunities to share their faith; for pursuing holiness in the fear of the Lord; and for the joy of the Lord to be their strength.

We pray for all students to finish their classes strong and rejoice in the graces you gave them this year. May you lead them into continued spiritual growth and service this summer.

Please provide comfort for those who are grieving the loss of loved ones or cherished dreams, healing for those who are sick, peace for those who are troubled, jobs for those un- or under-employed, reconciliation for those who are estranged, help for those who are weak, forgiveness for those who are weighed down by guilt, hope for those who are discouraged, welcome for those who are lonely, and grace for all of us to live with a strong and steady hope in Christ.

We ask for wisdom and grace for all who serve here: for pastors and staff, elders and deacons, growth group leaders and teachers, workers with children and youth, campus and international workers. Grant them compassion and zeal, good planning, and flexibility.

We intercede for marriages. Marriage is beautiful and hard. The enemy hates marriage and constantly attacks couples. Protect us from the evil one. Keep our selfish ways crucified. Enable us to love the honor of Christ more than we want our own comfort or pleasure. Give us discernment to identify the passions at war within us, which lead to conflict. Help us humble ourselves before you, resist the devil, and be exalted for your glory and our joy.

We pray for single people of all ages: for deep and satisfying fellowship with you and others; for holiness of body and mind; for a sense of value in this community of faith; and for joyful service to others.

Grant that we would be a people here at University Reformed Church marked by genuine holiness, reverent worship, warm hospitality, love for the truth, compassion for the needs of the poor, and a passionate desire to bring the gospel across the world, across the street, and across the hall.

We lift up the advancement of the gospel across the world, especially in the hard places. Give your sweet presence and mighty power to all who suffer persecution and trouble. Grant to missionaries and pastors protection, understanding of culture and language, passion for Christ, desire for souls to be saved, and an overarching love for the glory of God in all things.

"To God be the glory, great things he has done! So loved he the world that he gave us his Son; who yielded his life an atonement for sin, and opened the life-gate so we may go in!"[3] Amen and Amen!

———

"And so, from the day we heard, we have not ceased to pray for you, asking that you may be filled with the knowledge of his will in all spiritual wisdom and understanding, so as to walk in a manner worthy of the Lord, fully pleasing to him: bearing fruit in every good work and increasing in the knowledge of God; being strengthened with all power, according to his glorious might, for all endurance and patience with joy; giving thanks to the Father, who has qualified you to share in the inheritance of the saints in light. He has delivered us from the domain of darkness and transferred us to the kingdom of his beloved Son, in whom we have redemption, the forgiveness of sins" (Col. 1:9–14).

Father, we thank you that you teach us how to pray in your word. We pray now Paul's words for your church.

Fill us with knowledge of your will through the faithful hearing and reading of your word. Make us devoted to your word in personal and family devotions, in growth groups, and in Sunday sermons.

Give us spiritual wisdom and understanding through your Holy Spirit. Make us dependent on him. We won't see and hear and receive and rejoice and live unless your Spirit enables us.

3 Fanny J. Crosby, "To God Be the Glory," 1875.

Cause us to walk worthy of our calling in Christ through the gospel. May we experience the word of the cross as the greatest concentration of power in the universe. Help us, like Jesus, to hate wickedness in all its forms and to love righteousness, to hunger and thirst for it, and to pursue it with all our hearts.

May we grow every day in our knowledge of and delight in you. Show us the path of life and fill us with promised joy and pleasure in your presence. May we believe and cry from the heart, "Your love is better than anything this world could give to us or take away from us!"

We also pray for those suffering in our congregation, that you would strengthen them with all power, for all endurance and patience with joy. If some need to go through a season of sorrow, may they be like Paul, sorrowful yet always rejoicing in their faithful Savior and blessed hope. And so we pray for . . .

Those grieving loss of loved ones, health, a job, a relationship, or a cherished dream. May they grieve with the hope that anything good we lose here will be restored to overflowing in the resurrection.

Those in struggling marriages. They may feel they have good reasons to give up; give them better reasons to endure and fight for the glory of Christ.

Those with wayward children. Give them the comfort of their righteousness in Christ and the strength to pray and hope and love.

Those who long to be married and have children. Help them look beyond this world to the only marriage that lasts forever and to remember that to those whom God calls to singleness he promises better blessings than marriage and children.

Those who face unique challenges in their families. Let their deepest desires be fulfilled in your hard providences.

Those ignored or rejected or mocked because of their commitment to Jesus—may they rejoice and be glad that they are counted worthy to suffer for the name of Christ. We pray in the name of our precious Savior. Amen.

———

Our great God and Father, we lift to you in this Christmas season a world that is still in darkness and sin, a world that desperately needs the good news of a great light and a great joy.

We pray for missionaries laboring in hard places and ask that your unstoppable word would save many from sin and death. We pray for the people of the Philippines and other places where natural disasters, wars, poverty, and oppression have devastated lives and ask that you would provide relief and restoration in Jesus's name.

We pray for those in our own congregation who have suffered the loss of loved ones. We pray for those who face uncertain futures for their children, for those with wayward children and others who long for children—may Jesus be their strength, comfort, hope, and consolation.

We pray for the other churches in this area and ask for clear, gracious, winsome, Spirit-empowered proclamation of the gospel leading to transformed lives. Revive us again, that your people may rejoice in you. Show us your steadfast love and grant us your salvation.

Lord, make us all like the shepherds on the night Jesus was born and cause us to hear good news of great joy today. Make us like the magi and cause us to rejoice exceedingly with great joy because we have found our heart's desire in him. Make us like Mary and cause us to treasure all these things in our hearts and ponder them daily. And cause us to live lives of deep satisfaction, radiant joy, and sacrificial service. In Jesus's name. Amen.

———

"For if, because of one man's trespass, death reigned through that one man, much more will those who receive the abundance of grace and the free gift of righteousness reign in life through the one man Jesus Christ" (Rom. 5:17).

Lord, we know that sin and death always go together. Because of Adam's sin, death reigns. And there are many "little deaths" that precede the final death—loss of peace in our hearts and relationships, loss of health in our bodies, loss of dreams for the future, loss of material security, and loss of hope. We think of those who are chronically ill, those struggling with anxiety or depression, those in relational conflict, those who are lonely, those looking for work or who work in very hard circumstances. Please, Lord, give them comforting, healing, and hope-filled help.

Right now we all stretch out our hands and open our hearts to the abundance of grace and free righteousness that is ours in Christ. Teach us to rejoice in our sufferings. Teach us to hope for the day when sin and suffering will be no more.

Lord, we confess that our deepest grief is that we are not yet what we will be. We ache in the tension of the already and the not yet. We rejoice in our salvation but still groan under the burden of our flesh. We long to see Jesus and to become like him in his glory, to be finally and perfectly free from warfare with the world, flesh, and devil. We long for the glory, honor, and peace that you promise to those who do good. Strengthen us to do good, not in order to be saved, but because we have been saved—not in our own strength, but in the strength you provide. Build under our feet the solid rock of Romans 8:31–39:

> What then shall we say to these things? If God is for us, who can be against us? He who did not spare his own Son but gave him up for us all, how will he not also with him graciously give us all things? Who shall bring any charge against God's elect? It is God who justifies. Who is to condemn? Christ Jesus is the one who died—more than that, who was raised—who is at the right hand of God, who indeed is interceding for us. Who shall separate us from the love of Christ? Shall tribulation, or distress, or persecution, or famine, or nakedness, or danger, or sword? As it is written,
>
> "For your sake we are being killed all the day long;
>   we are regarded as sheep to be slaughtered."
>
> No, in all these things we are more than conquerors through him who loved us. For I am sure that neither death nor life, nor angels nor rulers, nor things present nor things to come, nor powers, nor height nor depth, nor anything else in all creation, will be able to separate us from the love of God in Christ Jesus our Lord.

Amen and Amen!

———

May God be gracious to us and bless us
  and make his face to shine upon us,
that your way may be known on earth,
  your saving power among all nations.
Let the peoples praise you, O God;
  let all the peoples praise you! (Ps. 67:1–3)

We love that you are gracious and merciful, Father, forgiving our sins, welcoming us in Christ, blessing us beyond our expectations: for this church and the denomination we serve in, for these beautiful facilities and grounds, for this family of brothers and sisters in Christ, for the glorious and messy work of the gospel.

We pray you would continue to show your kindness to us. Bless our pastors, our ministry and support staff. Bless each one of your people here with the health and strength and resources we need to take up our crosses and follow you. Bless us with many opportunities to serve and witness in Jesus's name.

We want your way known on the earth and your saving power among the nations. We thank you for the missionaries you have raised up from URC. Strengthen them with your power and fill them with your love so that they might proclaim Christ, serve with compassion, and lead many to saving faith.

We ask that you would comfort those who are suffering in the world today: victims of terrorism in France, Germany, Turkey, the United States, and other places; for victims of racial and ethnic oppression; for victims of natural disasters and poverty; and for victims of persecution in places like southern Mexico, Cuba, Pakistan, North Korea, Malawi, and Iran.

Let the nations be glad and sing for joy,
> for you judge the peoples with equity
> and guide the nations upon earth.
Let the peoples praise you, O God;
> let all the peoples praise you! (Ps. 67:4–5)

Father, we also pray for all the nations and all the peoples of North, Central, and South America, Europe and Asia, Africa, and the Middle East. May your gospel take root and flourish in every nation among every people group. May the grace of Christ liberate individuals and transform cultures. May leaders govern in righteousness. May businesses and industries provide needs with integrity. May educational institutions teach true knowledge. May churches be filled with born-again worshipers. Then the nations will be glad and sing for joy. And the joy of the Lord will be their strength and security.

Lord, we pray for the leaders of our country and the political candidates to seek the wisdom from above that begins with the fear of the Lord. Teach a culture that dishonors you in a thousand ways the fear of the Lord. Teach your church in America that too easily falls into cowardly isolation, judgmental criticism, or indifferent accommodation to be light and salt, to speak with a brokenhearted prophetic voice, and to raise high the cross of Christ.

The earth has yielded its increase;
> God, our God, shall bless us.
God shall bless us;
> let all the ends of the earth fear him! (Ps. 67:6–7)

Father, we know that when we pray your word, we pray your will. So we thank you that you have heard us and will answer. We thank you that your sovereign grace is irresistible and invincible. You will bless us and bless the world through us. You have exalted above all things your name and your word and have given Christ Jesus the name above all names. In that matchless name we pray. Amen.

———

Lord, we acknowledge that while the sufferings of this present age are not worth comparing with the glory that will be revealed to us, the world we live in is still full of anxiety, frustration, corruption, and groaning.

Hurricanes devastate cities, states, and even entire countries. Have mercy on us, Lord!

Terrorists threaten innocent ethnic groups and populations. Have mercy, Lord!

Racism seethes under the surface of our neighborhoods and communities. Have mercy, Lord!

Ambition and greed corrupt our governments. Have mercy, Lord!

Half-baked ideas and wholehearted foolishness infect our schools. Have mercy, Lord!

Self-righteousness and conflict weaken our churches. Have mercy, Lord!

(I'm going to suggest topics for prayer and allow time to pray silently.)

Lord, in your great mercy, would you heal all who are sick in body, comfort all who are discouraged in spirit, give wisdom to all who are confused in mind, stir up all who are sluggish in worship, deliver all who are stuck in sin, empower all who are engaged in gospel ministry, and grant peace to all who are fearful in heart.

We pray in Jesus's name. Amen.

———

"But we have this treasure in jars of clay, to show that the surpassing power belongs to God and not to us" (2 Cor. 4:7).

Father, the treasure of the gospel is beyond our wildest dreams, but we carry it in ordinary and frail lives.

So we pray for those who feel afflicted in every way: sickness, relentless stresses in the home and workplace, broken relationships, financial strain, marital or parental anguish, besetting sins. Thank you that by the resurrection power of Christ, they are afflicted but not crushed. Strengthen, encourage, and lift them up.

We pray for those perplexed: struggling with doubts, hard decisions, overwhelming circumstances. Thank you that though they are perplexed, through the wisdom of Christ they are not driven to despair. Enlighten them with your perspective, understanding, and direction.

We pray for brothers and sisters who are experiencing the kind of persecution we don't really understand: for the pastor who was finally released from prison in Bangladesh; for Christians in Mexico, who have been forced out of their homes and farmland; for a church in Sri Lanka whose worship service was threatened and stopped; and for countless other Christians who daily pay a steep price for faithfully following Jesus. Thank you that you have not and never will forsake them. Let them know that they are not forgotten, that your eye is upon them, that your hand protects them, and that your plan for their good will never fail. Strengthen them with the love and power of Jesus to remain faithful and grant them relief and release through your providential hand.

We pray for those struck down by accident, war, terrorism, and natural disasters. Thank you that they are not destroyed and that they have better possessions and a more secure life awaiting them if they trust in Christ. Provide relief and restoration through government help, the kindness of neighbors, and the works and witness of your people.

May the life and glory of Christ be manifested in our mortal bodies and ordinary lives as we walk with him through the trials of this life. And may our sharing in his sufferings bring comfort and salvation to our neighbors and to the nations. In Jesus's name. Amen.

———

We thank you, Father, that though you are high and lifted up and dwell in unapproachable light, you also care for the poor and needy, for those who are willing to humble themselves before you and seek your help. We are those needy people this morning, Lord, and so we come humbly in the name of Jesus.

We lift up our mortal bodies to you, Lord. Some struggle with chronic pain or sickness or disability. Some are feeling the downward drag of aging and experiencing various ailments that they never had to deal with when younger. Some are facing or recovering from surgery or cancer treatments. In all these weaknesses and afflictions, Lord, have mercy. Send forth your word in Jesus's name and bring healing and help and hope.

We lift up our souls to you, Lord. Each one of us daily battles against stubborn weaknesses and besetting sins. Remind us, as Paul said, that our old selves were crucified with Christ in order that the body of sin might be brought to nothing and that we would no longer be slaves to sin. Help us, for your name's sake, to hate and put to death all our many ways of mistrusting you, of loving ourselves, of craving comfort or success or approval from others. Help us to put to death all the routine ways we exploit others to get what we want, all the false refuges we seek, and all the ways we turn your good gifts into destructive gods.

We lift up our church to you, Lord. Give a common gospel vision to pastors, staff, elders, and ministry leaders. Equip us for every-member ministry with the power, gifts, and fruit of the Holy Spirit. Anoint our preaching and teaching, discipling and counseling, men's and women's ministries, youth and college ministries, mercy and international ministries. Give us grace to effectively connect, equip, and serve in the power of the gospel. Grant us common vision, unified worship, and cooperative outreach to the Lansing area and the ends of the earth.

Finally, we lift up our persecuted brothers and sisters to you, Lord. Though they are often forgotten and suffer alone, your word tells us to remember those who are in prison as though we were in prison with them and to remember all those who are mistreated for the name of Christ. We pray for the suffering church all over the world, especially for a young woman in the Arabian peninsula who was put under house arrest by her own family after revealing she had become a Christian. We pray for the churches in northern

Ethiopia who are facing strong opposition and have had to close their doors. We pray for a pastor in China who was sentenced to nine years in prison. We pray for Algerian Christians seeking to remain faithful as authorities move to shut down their churches.

Strengthen these dear brothers and sisters, Lord. Remind them of the privilege of suffering for Jesus's sake and fill their hearts with love for you and for their persecutors. Use persecution to strengthen your church and grant them relief and peace in your good time.

Though we your people walk in the midst of trouble, you preserve our lives. You will fulfill your purpose for each one of us: to conform us to the image of Christ and to take us home to his glory and joy. Your steadfast love endures forever, O Lord. Do not forsake us, the work of your hands. Amen.

11

Composite Prayers

JOY TO THE WORLD! the Lord is come:
let earth receive her King;
let every heart prepare him room,
and heav'n and nature sing.[1]

Lord, how this world is starved for joy and seeks it in tinsel treasures and poisonous pleasures! Thank you that when you sent Jesus, you sent the only real and lasting joy.

With great anticipation and hope we joyfully receive Christ now. We have prepared our hearts and once again receive him as our Savior from sin, Lord of life, lover of our souls, our closest friend, brother in the fellowship of suffering, and as the very meaning and purpose of our lives. We have sung your praises and we sing in our hearts now—"Joy to the world! The Lord is come!"

Joy to the earth! The Savior reigns:
let men their songs employ;

1   Isaac Watts, "Joy to the Word," 1719.

while fields and floods, rocks, hills, and plains
repeat the sounding joy.

We praise you, Lord, that the Savior reigns. The stone that the builders rejected has become the chief cornerstone. The suffering servant has borne our sorrows and griefs and sicknesses and pains. The curse-bearer has become the blessing-giver. The sun of righteousness has risen. Thank you that the joy of our salvation is not only for us but also for extended family, neighbors, coworkers—for the whole world. You call us to go across the street, across the aisle, across racial divides, and across the world to bring the joy of our salvation.

We praise you that the salvation that Jesus brings impacts the entire creation—fields and floods, rocks, hills, and plains repeat the sounding joy. The oceans will roar, the trees of the field will clap their hands, the mountains will bow down when the King of glory comes. One day every knee will bow before Jesus and every blade of grass will be renewed to bring praise to him.

No more let sins and sorrows grow,
nor thorns infest the ground;
he comes to make his blessings flow
far as the curse is found.

Lord, we live in the time between the first and second coming of Christ. You have saved us, but we still await the perfection of that salvation. You have given us Christ's righteousness, but not yet perfected spirits; your Spirit to indwell us, but not yet spiritual imperishable bodies; hope, but not yet the blessed hope of seeing

Christ face to face; the foretaste of heaven, but not yet the river of life that flows from your throne.

Lord, help us each day to cast off every weight of sorrow that distracts and to lay aside every weight of sin that drags us down. Help us to see and hate and put off our sins of laziness, hypocrisy, pride, control, fear, lust, gossip, meanness, apathy, worldliness, double-mindedness, and disloyalty. These sins dishonor you, wound others, degrade us, and put off unbelievers.

Lord, let the blessings of your gospel flow as far as the curse is found—to all those who have lost loved ones, those in troubled marriages, those with disabled and wayward children, those who feel trapped in chronic physical, mental, or spiritual pain, and those who long to be married or to have children. There is much brokenness in the world, Lord. Thank you that nothing is impossible for you. Thank you that you promise to be with us and sustain and protect and deliver now, and you promise to wipe away every tear when Christ returns.

> He rules the world with truth and grace,
> and makes the nations prove
> the glories of his righteousness
> and wonders of his love.

All glory to you, Lord, who rules the world in truth and grace. We pray for our country: for a smooth transition to a new presidency; for wisdom and wise counselors for our president; for compassion and justice for all; for the end of racial and religious hostilities; for spiritual revival; for unity, purity, peace, and power in the body of Christ.

Finally, we pray for the nations: for leaders to seek your wisdom and righteousness, for the glory of Christ to cover the persecuted church, for peace in Syria, Iraq, and other troubled places. Lord Jesus, you have come, you sit at the right hand of the Father, and you will come again. Help us all believe, receive, rejoice, live, and give the glories of your righteousness and wonders of your love. Amen!

Lord Jesus Christ, we address you this morning as the radiance of your Father's infinite glory and the exact imprint of his holy nature. There is no one like you, Lord. We gladly acknowledge that we cannot know the Father or come to him apart from you. We stagger at the reality that all the fullness of deity dwells in you, the God-man. As we offer our prayers to you this morning, we also worship the Father who sent you and the Spirit who reveals you.

We thank you, Lord Jesus, that you are the sun of righteousness and that you have risen with healing in your wings for all who believe. We love that your righteousness brings healing to our lives. How we need your healing touch in:

Marriages and families. Tensions exist between frustrated husbands and wives, frustrated parents and children, and frustrated extended family members. Bring peace and reconciliation where there is stress and conflict.

Workplaces. Many face tedious work, demanding employers, or unhelpful coworkers.

Our bodies. We suffer from minor colds and serious physical disabilities. Heal those suffering and give grace and strength to caregivers.

Our souls. Heal our sin-sickness. Free us from all the ways we deceive ourselves and others, all the ways we enslave ourselves and manipulate others, and all the ways we more resemble the father of lies than the Father of lights.

We praise you, Jesus, that you are the Lion of Judah, that you rule over heaven and earth, and that the scepter will never depart from your hand.

While you are gentle and lowly, you are also a fierce and mighty enemy of all evil. We live in a world that is increasingly hostile to grace, truth, and righteousness.

Our hearts are grieved at random violence to African-American brothers and sisters gunned down while they were studying the Bible. Have mercy.

Our hearts are angry at the foolishness and arrogance of Supreme Court justices who ignore our country's heritage, fabricating Constitutional arguments to redefine marriage and institutionalize sin. Have mercy.

Lion of Judah, would you roar through our world and country your message of judgment and salvation—urgent warnings of wrath and tearful pleas for repentance. We know you take pleasure not in the death of the wicked but in the repentance and salvation of sinners.

We adore you, Lord Jesus, as the rose of Sharon, the lily of the valley, the fairest of ten thousand, the bridegroom of the church.

In this world of tinsel treasures, ravish our hearts with the beauty of your holiness. Speak to us as we worship: "Arise, my love, [my church], my beautiful one, / and come away, / for behold, the winter is past; / the rain is over and gone. / The flowers appear on the earth, / the time of singing has come" (Song 2:10–12).

In this world of innumerable voices, distractions, and temptations, make us people of one thing, like David, who said, "One thing have I asked of the LORD" (Ps. 27:4).

Help us to tremble at Paul's words: "If anyone has no love for the Lord, let him be accursed" (1 Cor. 16:22). "No love for the Lord" is not a small thing. Help us repent of the terrible sin of having little or no love for you, who are altogether lovely.

Finally, Lord Jesus, we bow before you as our beloved King, Creator, and Master of the universe, ruler of heaven and earth.

We long for the day when every knee will bow and tongue confess that you are Lord, when all rebellion is crushed beneath the mighty weight of your glory.

We long for the day when we will see you as you really are: no longer in a mirror dimly, no longer in our sin-distorted imaginations. Then we will be made like you in your glory. We will not only see but also share in the glory you had before the foundation of the world.

But we're not there yet. So as we rest and worship today and go back to work tomorrow, we recommit ourselves to be your willing servants. There is no greater joy than to serve you. We know that our greatest freedom is in being your bond slaves, that the way to greatness is the way of sacrificial love. Give each of us grace to faithfully serve in the place you have us—husbands and wives, moms and dads, brothers and sisters, employers and employees, teachers and students, friends and coworkers, leaders and congregation, young and old, healthy and sick, weak and strong—each one of us has an important part to play, a commission to fulfill, a place to serve. Oh, how we want to be found faithful when you return and to hear you say, "Well done, good and faithful servant. . . . Enter into the joy of your master" (Matt. 25:21, 23). May it be so for your glory. Amen.

———

"I bow down toward your holy temple / and give thanks to your name for your steadfast love and your faithfulness, / for you have exalted above all things / your name and your word" (Ps. 138:2).

Lord, how we love your covenant name: Yahweh, "I AM WHO I AM." Jesus, "God saves." We immerse ourselves in the majesty of your names in Scripture, delight ourselves in your character, and strengthen our faith in your mighty acts.

You are Yahweh Nissi, the Lord Our Banner. We praise you, Lord, that you deliver us from the enslaving power of the world, flesh, and devil so we are free to serve you without fear in holiness and righteousness all our days. We praise you that Jesus has put our flesh to death and raised us to new life, crucified us to the seduction of the world, delivered us from the tyranny of the devil, and even taken the sting out of death.

You are Yahweh Rapha, the Lord Our Healer. Lord, we tremble at the mystery of Jesus bearing our sins and sufferings on the cross so that by his wounds we might be healed. We praise you that you not only forgive all our sins but heal all our diseases—either in this life or the next.

You are Yahweh Rohi, the Lord Our Shepherd. You guide us wisely and lead us fearlessly. What a comfort that you know the way home; that you are the way home; that all we have needed your hand has provided; that even when we walk through the valley of the shadow of death, we need fear no evil. What amazing love that you call us each by name, lay down your life for us, and promise never to lose even one of us.

You are Yahweh Tsidkenu, the Lord Our Righteousness, and Yahweh M'kaddesh, the Lord Who Sanctifies. Thank you, Lord, that as we embrace Jesus as Savior and Lord, we receive a triple blessing: Christ as our forgiveness to free us from guilt; Christ as our righteousness to free us from condemnation; and Christ as our power to free us from corruption.

You are Yahweh Shalom, the Lord Our Peace. Lord, this world is often characterized more by chaos than peace. We are at war with ourselves, one another, and you. We praise you that Jesus is the great reconciler; he breaks down the dividing walls of hostility and brings compassion, justice, and wholeness.

You are Yahweh Jireh, the Lord Our Provider. Your greatest provision is Jesus our sin-bearing substitute. On the mountain of Moriah you stopped Abraham from sacrificing his son, but on the same mountain you did not stay your own hand. By your will Jesus was plunged into darkness so we could enjoy the light of life. He was undone so we might become new creations. He was abandoned so we might be welcomed. He died so we might live forever. Thank for you the gospel, Lord! And thank you that not only did you not spare your own Son, but you have promised to give us all things with him.

You are Yahweh Shammah, the Lord Who Is There. This is best of all, Lord. You are the best gift of the gospel. All other blessings are good insofar as they reveal your glory and lead us to enjoy you forever. This is the message of the Bible: Immanuel, God with us. *"I will be your God and you will be my people."* What more could we dream of or desire? One thing we ask of you, Lord, and that will we seek—that we may dwell in your house forever, gaze upon your beauty, and inquire in your temple. Whom have we in heaven but you, Lord? There is nothing on earth we desire besides you. Even so, come, Lord Jesus; not only come, but come quickly. Amen and amen.

———

"For the grace of God has appeared, bringing salvation for all people" (Titus 2:11).

We love and praise you, heavenly Father, for the glory of your grace that actually appeared in person two thousand years ago in an obscure Middle Eastern country. We marvel at the grace of Jesus as an infant, young boy, adolescent, and man. Perfect holiness; perfect kindness; perfect wisdom; perfect power; perfect God; and perfect man.

This grace we see in your Son is the radiance of your glory and the image of your character. And from his grace, your grace, we have all received grace upon grace upon grace.

This grace is amazing. It saves wretches. It brings lost children home. It opens blind eyes. It both teaches us to fear and relieves our fears. It brings us safe through all the dangers, toils, and snares of life. It promises ten thousand times ten thousand ages of joyfully singing your praises and serving your kingdom in heaven.

This grace is costly. It cost Christ the lowly birth, the blood of circumcision, the flight to Egypt, the thirty years of obscurity, the sinner's baptism, the sinless life, the constant grief and sorrow, the vicarious suffering, the cursed death, and the three days in the tomb. But he rose triumphantly from the dead, overcoming every obstacle to eternal life for all who believe.

This grace brings salvation for all people—rich and poor, respectable and despised, strong and weak, influential and unknown. This salvation is for anyone who recognizes that this is your world and that he or she has not honored you as you deserve and who turns to Christ to believe in and receive him.

"[This grace trains] us to renounce ungodliness and worldly passions, and to live self-controlled, upright, and godly lives in the present age" (Titus 2:12).

Thank you, Lord, that your grace not only teaches us but disciples us to say no to wrong ways of thinking and to corrupt desires, and to actions that make you look small, unimportant, and of little account

Help us, Lord, to recognize where we are poor, blind, naked, wretched, and pitiful; to come to you for forgiveness and new life; to desire your glory more than nice houses, nice children, nice jobs, and nice lives. Help us to live lives that make people wonder why we don't live for comfort, success, and self-esteem.

Grace trains us also to wait for "our blessed hope, the appearing of the glory of our great God and Savior Jesus Christ" (Titus 2:13).

Each one of us hopes for something, Lord: an iPhone, car, boyfriend, spouse, child, job, or house. We hope for relief from pain, a happier marriage, the kids to move out, or a comfortable retirement.

But you hold out to us a blessed hope, a happy hope, a lasting hope, a radiant hope, a never-ending hope: the appearing of our God and Savior Jesus Christ. Only Jesus can heal the horrible brokenness, bring true justice, satisfy our deepest longings, remove the curse of sin and suffering, and make all things new.

We need you more than the air we breathe, Lord Jesus! We wait! We watch! We worship! We cry, "Maranatha! Come, Lord Jesus!"

This Jesus "gave himself for us to redeem us from all lawlessness and to purify for himself a people for his own possession who are zealous for good works" (Titus 2:14).

Lord, we know we are not home yet. Today we groan in the pains of childbirth looking forward to you wiping away every tear. Tomorrow will begin a challenging week as some grapple with poor health, frustrating jobs, unruly emotions, and old temptations. Have mercy on us, Lord.

Thank you, Lord Jesus, that the real heavy lifting belongs not to us but to you—*you* gave yourself for us; *you* delivered us from the guilt and power of sin; *you* have washed us clean and made us presentable to the Father; *you* give us the eternal security of being your own possession; *you* move us to be zealous for good works.

Holy Spirit, help us fix our eyes on Jesus tomorrow. Help us draw on his grace moment by moment. Then help us look around to see who God has put in our lives to love and lead us into the good works you have prepared beforehand for us to do. We pray this in Jesus's name. Amen.

———

Heavenly Father, we praise you that you are our Creator, sustainer, Redeemer, and King, that these titles are perfectly manifested through your Son Jesus, and that the benefits of these titles come to us through the ministry of the Holy Spirit. All glory to the triune God: Blessed Father! Precious Jesus! Holy Spirit!

Father, you sent Jesus to give us life. David describes this life in Psalm 16: "Preserve me, O God, for in you I take refuge. / I say to the Lord, "You are my Lord; / I have no good apart from you" (Ps. 16:1–2).

Thank you, Lord, that you invite us to take refuge in you and find our ultimate good in you at all times. Thank you for your constant protection and provision.

We pray for all those who need your protection and provision: for the poor and homeless in the Lansing area; for women and children who are neglected or abused; for the unemployed or underemployed; for those trapped in oppression or addiction; for victims of terrorism or persecution. Be their refuge and satisfy them with good things as they call on your name.

"As for the saints in the land, they are the excellent ones, in whom is all my delight" (Ps. 16:3).

We thank you, Father, for providing us with the fellowship and accountability of the church family. Thank you for the delight we have in brothers and sisters in Christ, for the mutual encouragement we enjoy, and for many opportunities we have to study your word and pray and serve together.

But Lord, we know not every person experiences this life-giving fellowship. We pray for those who are new to URC and haven't yet found a warm welcome. Help us to reach out to invite newcomers into our conversations and, more importantly, into our lives. We pray for those of all ages who are lonely; for those who struggle with English language or culture; for those who are far from home and feel disoriented; for those who have a hard time in social situations and stay on the fringe; and for those who even feel unworthy of friendship. May all who pass through these doors be loved and welcomed even as you have loved and welcomed us.

"The sorrows of those who run after another god shall multiply; / their drink offerings of blood I will not pour out / or take their names on my lips. / The LORD is my chosen portion and my cup; / you hold my lot. / The lines have fallen for me in pleasant places; / indeed, I have a beautiful inheritance" (Ps. 16:4–6).

Thank you for your clear warnings and bright promises, Father. Those who chase gods of comfort, success, pleasure, achievement, control, or anything other than your glory will ultimately have great sorrow and eternal loss. We praise you that you are generous beyond our wildest dreams and offer us the true riches of your heavenly wisdom, which is Christ himself. His love is better than silver or gold, and he brings life, honor, peace, and joy through the gospel.

Keep us from craving and pursuing what the world seeks. Save us from keeping company with those who will distract us from our first love and lead us astray. Give us hearts that quickly recognize sinful attractions and turn away from these to what really satisfies.

"I bless the LORD who gives me counsel; / in the night also my heart instructs me. / I have set the LORD always before me; / because he is at my right hand, I shall not be shaken" (Ps. 16:7–8).

We bless you, Lord Jesus, that you are our Wonderful Counselor. You know human nature and the pains and pleasures of life better than we do. You feel our very weaknesses, were tempted in every way, and invite us to the throne of grace in times of need. Thank you for the wise counsel you give us through Scripture and the Holy Spirit, who is able to help us correctly interpret and wisely respond to all our struggles. Thank you that you are an indestructible rock to keep us steady when the world is shaking and crumbling around us.

Lord, we pray for all who are struggling with hard situations: for troubled marriages, wayward children, great fears, and grievous losses. We pray for those struggling with chronic illness and pain. And we pray for each one of us who desperately needs your wisdom and grace every hour. Be our counselor. Be our rock.

"Therefore my heart is glad, and my whole being rejoices; / my flesh also dwells secure. / For you will not abandon my soul to Sheol, / or let your holy one see corruption. / You make known to me the path of life; / in your presence there is fullness of joy; / at your right hand are pleasures forevermore" (Ps. 16:9–11).

Lord, we rejoice in this beautiful summary of gospel hope: gladness and security, assurance of future grace, guidance on the path of life, fullness of joy, and pleasures forevermore. All this is ours because Jesus became our sin so we could become the righteousness of God. Jesus suffered so we could be healed. Jesus became our curse so we could be blessed with the Holy Spirit. Jesus died so we could live forever in your presence. Hallelujah, what a Savior! Help us this week to enjoy and share the blessings you have given and to wait patiently for the full measure of blessings to come. Amen.

General Index

Abraham, 93, 160
abundance, 84, 87, 100, 115, 120, 144
acrostic psalms, 51
ACTS (acronym), 30n1
Adam, 31
addiction, 164
"ad lib" prayers, 68–69
adoption, 64, 99
adoration, 17, 19, 20, 22, 30, 31–32, 47–48, 71–74, 83–104
adultery, 32, 108
affliction, 78, 99–100, 151
Africa, 132
African Americans, 157
alcohol, 24
Algeria, 152
allusions, 24, 38
already and the not yet, 144
Anderson, Jon, 40
anxiety, 121, 144
apathy, 135, 155
apostles, 11, 17, 92
Apostles' Creed, 47, 65
armor of God, 123–24, 137
Asaph, 62–63
Asia, 130, 132

assurance of pardon, 33, 71, 75, 76, 166
Athanasian Creed, 65
atheism, 117
Augustine, 102

banality, 50
Bangladesh, 149
baptism, 71
Baxter, Richard, 39n5, 40
Beatitudes, 76
beauty, 88, 92
Begg, Alistair, 16n1
benedictions, 30, 71
betrayal, 32
Bible, 67. *See also* Scripture
Bible Christians, 38
biblical language, 24
blasphemy, 32
blessing, 57
bodies, 156
brokenness, 124, 155

cadence, 69
call to worship, 30, 71
Calvin, John, 20–21, 30n1
Carson, D. A., 56

foolishness, 113
forgetfulness, 130
forgiveness, 33, 75, 76, 98, 101,
    109, 111, 113, 115, 159
fornication, 24
Frame, John, 45
France, 146
freedom, 69, 158
frustration, 124

genealogies, 63
Germany, 146
Getty, Keith, 47
gifts, 110, 134
gladness, 166
glory, 102
God
    beauty of, 31–32
    glory of, 59
    holiness of, 32, 52, 88, 116, 118,
        157
    love of, 52
    promises of, 18, 165
gospel, 24, 33, 55–59, 68, 76, 78,
    94, 133, 140, 151, 166
gossip, 108, 155
grace, 84, 161, 162
gravitas, 32
grief, 121, 139, 142, 166
"grocery list" syndrome, 34
guilt, 105, 119, 139

Haiti, 128
healing, 34
heart, sins of, 75
Helopoulos, Jason, 18
Henry, Matthew, 22–23, 30n1,
    38n3, 47–48
historical liturgies, 30n1, 62
holiness, 32, 52, 88, 116, 118, 119,
    139, 140, 157, 159, 161

Holy Spirit
    as Comforter, 22, 91, 92, 93
    gift of, 90
    illumination of, 21, 102
    including in prayer, 24
    praying directly to, 46–47
    wisdom of, 141, 165
hope, 83, 162, 166
hospitality, 140
human intellect, 102
humility, 85–86
hymns, 30, 71
hypocrisy, 155

idolatry, 23, 59, 96, 108, 110, 114,
    127, 135
illness, 78, 125, 144, 150, 154, 166
illumination, 30
immanence, 52
improvisation, 40
incarnation, 87, 89, 136
indifference, 130, 147
inheritance, 83–84
"inside out," 78
Iran, 130, 135, 146
Iraq, 128
irreverent prayer, 50–51, 52

jazz, 40
Jesus Christ
    glory of, 58–59, 68, 94–95
    as mediator, 97
    on prayer, 15–17
    resurrection of, 83, 85, 162
    righteousness of, 57, 113, 123
jobs, 78, 133
Johnson, Terry L., 23n12, 38n2
joy, 95, 112, 126, 153
judgment, 90, 99
justice, 155, 163
justification, 64

Scripture Index